Catholic Traditions in Crafts

Catholic Traditions in Crafts

Ann Ball

Our Sunday Visitor Publishing Division
Our Sunday Visitor, Inc.
Huntington, Indiana 46750

Dedication

With gratitude to the "girls" now in heaven who taught me the joy of making things, this book is dedicated to the "girls" in my family: Julie, Julianne, Joanna, Danielle, Courtney, and Victoria. And to Lorraine, who makes things for me all the time and who says that a little of her love for doing this came from me. Also to Mary Ellen and Bebe, who helped so much in testing the directions for the crafts in this book.

Contents

Introduction (and Advice!)

"Mama, I'm so glad you raised us the way you did !" My twenty-seven-year-old called to me from the kitchen, and as any normal mother would do in the face of a remark like that, I raced to see what could have caused her to say such a thing.

In the kitchen, Joanna was busily putting the finishing touches on a craft project she was making. When she saw the look on my face, she said, "When I was young, sometimes I used to resent the fact that you made everything. I envied the kids who could go in a store and just buy what they wanted. I didn't realize then that we were probably often short of money. But it wasn't until I began to make things myself that I began to see how wonderful it is to be able to make things. And my friends like the things I make them!"

Joanna had discovered the special feeling of accomplishment people feel when they create something; often a work of art springs from ordinary materials. Her friends undoubtedly like what she makes because they realize that she puts part of herself into each handcrafted item.

Since I was a child, I have enjoyed working with my hands. Messes were my forte. My sister was the perfect, neat, girl-child. Her room was filled with pink frills and stuffed animals. My room, on the other hand, was spartan. The floors were most often covered with newspapers, rather than carpet, to catch the paint dribbles. Instead of perfume bottles and delicate china knick-knacks, my bureau held glue, brushes, and crayons.

My mother was a teacher, and art materials were readily available at our house. In addition, my grandmother lived nearby with her sister, and their other sister was a frequent visitor. For me, it was like having three grandmothers. Each of the "the girls" made things — cooking, needlework, all types of crafts. Aunt Minnie introduced me to needlework — crochet, crewel, and huck weaving became my favorites. MaMa Dear let me cook and create in the kitchen. Aunt Ora did everything by hand from oil painting to making her own bullets. Best of all, they had a special room for crafts and I was allowed to work in it with them, with the only proviso that I not waste and that I clean up after myself.

In the post-war era I grew up in, the family budget didn't allow for many extras. Just as Joanna later discovered, making the things we needed was often as much necessity as pleasure. Some of my prettiest dresses as a child were made from flour sacks, hand-decorated by one of my great-aunts. Gifts for our friends were often made from leftovers or found items. We recycled before it was popular.

On purpose I tried to introduce my children to the joys of making things themselves. I treasure my daughter's first ceramic, made when she was only three, and my son's first real painting — just like a boy, he picked a bug to paint!

This love of working with my hands has apparently rubbed off on my children, for which I am grateful. Not only does my daughter create much better craft projects than I do, but in her travels with the U.S. Air Force, she has sought out and sent me beautiful handmade items from many cultures. A large part of my son's job in the Coast Guard is making or repairing things.

Our family tradition of handwork is passing from generation to generation. My sister was fortunate to marry a man who can fix or repair almost anything. Their daughter, my niece Julianne, inherited his manual dexterity. Her husband Curt builds things like furniture beautifully, and her mother-in-law also has taught her many crafts projects. At eight, my great-niece, Courtney, is getting quite clever at crafts projects herself. During a recent visit from my niece's family, Julianne and Curt decided to go to the ballgame; their son Jeremy decided to go, too; and Courtney stayed home with me. When I asked her if she felt like doing something a little "artsy craftsy," she responded, "I just thought you might say that!" Whereupon she rummaged in her suitcase and brought out a tiny glue gun. She had come prepared!

Why Make Crafts?

Throughout history, humans have made what we needed for everyday life. In addition to making things functional, we added decorations to make them aesthetically pleasing. Many objects have been made for religious purposes. These are among the most beautiful and carefully made objects from any culture. Even in today's modern world, with factory-produced goods, there is a place for handmade goods. Nowhere is this more true than in the celebration of the Christian religion. Traditionally, Catholics have taken the best of what they had to offer and brought them to their religious celebrations.

Today, because of the busy schedules kept by many Americans, some of the traditional crafts are dying out. In this book, I have tried to simplify some of these so that the reader can gain at least an idea of the original process, even in the face of a limited time period. I have tried to include projects simple enough for any novice, and projects practical enough to be used with groups such as schools and CCD classes. An annotated bibliography will help the serious crafter locate directions for more advanced and difficult projects. Most of the materials and supplies used in the projects in this book should be readily available throughout the United States. For those readers who live in rural areas, I have tried to include the addresses of mail order sources for supplies not available locally. Some projects included are suitable for young children; others are more complicated. Some are good for use with groups; others are handled best by a single artist. All projects are structured to help bring the living Church more deeply into our daily lives.

A Story of String

One of the first craft projects I created for this book was a string rosary. To make it, I used nylon twine from a spool in my garage. Knowing that I needed to use string that was readily available to the readers of this book, I looked on the spool for the type and size of string. It was unmarked. I then began to search for this type of string in the stores. The craft store had lots of nylon twine, but none exactly like the type I had used for my prototype. I checked the grocery store, the drug store, and a number of hardware stores. No luck. Next I tried the specialty yarn shops and model shops. Finally I became convinced that my twine wasn't made any more.

I was griping about this to one of the "big" kids at lunch and he asked to see the rosary. "Ms. B.," he said, "you can buy all you want of that string at the sporting goods store in the fishing equipment department." He was correct — my string, available in a variety of colors, was sold right next to the wiggly bait, and at a much more reasonable price than the next most useful type I had found at the craft store.

The pony beads used for the rosary have a similar story. I could find large packages of them for sale at the craft store. If I were making the rosary with a CCD class, this would be quite economical. But I only needed a few beads, and at the craft store small quantities were expensive. Fortunately, while I was at the dollar store, I noticed that in the hair-bow section the same beads were sold very cheaply!

Part of the fun of making handcrafts is finding the best and cheapest place to buy the supplies. Throughout the text I will include hints on places to look for supplies, and there is a section in the back of the book with addresses where you can mail-order supplies if you cannot find them locally. Happy hunting!

Tool Talk

In this book, I have tried to include crafts that do not call for exotic or expensive tools. Here are some things you'll need:

- A basic set of acrylic paints
- A jar of gesso prepping plaster (obtain from an art supply or craft store)
- A hot-glue gun (the type with a trigger is preferable)
- A saw (obtain a small, inexpensive coping saw at the hardware or dollar store)
- An electric engraver (sometimes called an electric pencil; also obtained at the hardware store)
- Scissors, white glue, a hammer (usually already part of your household equipment)

Safety First

Please use and store all tools safely. The hot-glue gun is one of the most dangerous of all tools if you are not careful when handling it. Obtain a piece of scrap board to use as a pad for your gun; unplug it when you aren't using it. If you dribble some of the glue on your fingers, do *not try* and pull it off! Instead, immediately immerse your hand in cold water. Pulling hot glue off will bring skin with it and continue the burn; immersing it stops the burn.

When using the electric engraver, always wear safety glasses to prevent metal or glass chips from flying and hitting your eye.

Patterns

There's always more than one way to skin a cat — and the patterns in this book prove that old saying. Patterns, when needed, are provided on a grid. They can be enlarged using old-fashioned graph paper. An easier way, however, is enlarge it on a copy machine. If you don't have access to a copier at work or home, take the pattern to your local quick print shop and ask them to help you. The cost should be less than a dollar for one copy. Your local library also may have a low-cost copier that enlarges. For a detailed explanation on enlarging patterns, see page 179.

Spray Away

Almost everyone *thinks* they can spray paint; almost no one really does it well! It's simple, if you follow a few hints and have lots of patience. The abundance of quick-dry paints proves that most people want to rush things.

When you prepare to spray paint, shake the can well for the time called for on the label. Under-mixed paint will streak and take longer to dry. Spray in light coats the proper distance from your project. If you spray too closely, the paint will run. If you are painting over markers or other types of colored paint, a first coat that is too heavy will cause the colors to bleed. Ten light coats are far better than two heavy ones. Buy quality paints for most projects, especially when you need a clear spray. When you have finished painting for the session, hold the can upside down and spray for a few seconds to clear the hole.

Brand X

For some of the crafts in this book, I have used "brand name" products. Hopefully, these will be readily available in your area; if not, see the the mail order supply list on page 181.

When a product is named by brand, it is because: 1) I know it works; 2) I believe it is a safe product to use; or 3) I don't know of any other product like it. For example, I don't know of any other clay that works like Crayola's Model Magic modeling compound, which hardens to a non-shrinking, flexible texture.

This does not mean that you can't use Brand X! For example, as a child, all of my crayons were Crayolas. Thus, I came to call all wax crayons "Crayolas." This is incorrect; wax crayon is the generic term. For projects in this book that call for wax crayons you can use any brand you have on hand.

A lot of the fun of making things is in the innovations you create yourself. The publisher and I would appreciate hearing from you regarding any difficulty you may find in obtaining products and supplies used in this book, and of any substitutes that you find work well for you.

Ann Ball

The Christmas Season

The celebration that begins the liturgical year is Advent, a movable observance beginning on the Sunday closest to the last day in November. The season precedes and prepares the way for Christmas. As a preparatory season, Advent started in Rome during the sixth century with a joyful character; later, the Frankish influence gave it a penitential character. By the twelfth century, a compromise made it a time of joyful penance.

In the year 312, under the Emperor Constantine, the Church was at last free from persecution. About the middle of the fourth century, she established a special feast to commemorate the birth of Christ. In 386, St. John Chrysostom wrote that Pope Julian had made an extensive investigation of the correct birthday of Christ and found that the Western churches all considered December 25 to be the Nativity date, although the Eastern churches claimed January 6. Other opinions abounded, variously setting the date in March, April, May, or September. To end the controversy, and basing his opinion on the majority, Pope Julian decreed the feast for December 25.

By the Middle Ages, this feast acquired the popular name of Christmas (Mass of Christ). It rapidly became one of the most joyous feasts of the liturgical year and was celebrated happily in the churches and in the home.

From the early Middle Ages, the twelve days from the Nativity of Our Lord to the Epiphany (January 6) were kept as a festive season. Although these twelve days are dominated by Christmas, they also contain other liturgical feasts to increase the spirit of joy and celebration.

Throughout the history of the season, handcrafts have always made a large contribution to the festivities in the form of decorations and gifts. Each ethnic heritage has special crafts dedicated to this season. Entire books can be, and have been, written on the crafts of Christmas. It is well outside the scope of this book to do anything other than present a sampling of the thousands of crafts used in the celebration of Christmas.

Luminarios

The Mexican custom of *los luminarios* has crossed the border and many places now decorate with these festive lights, symbolizing the Advent of the Christ Child. During Advent and Christmas, the hilly city of El Paso, Texas, sparkles with the *luminarios* set out in hundreds of front yards. Traditionally, the *luminarios* are made by partially filling a paper sack with sand, placing a small candle inside, and lighting it. The sacks are placed along the walkways leading to the homes. Unfortunately, long periods of burning use quite a lot of candles, and the wind plays tricks by blowing them out time and again.

Our friend Army Emmot created a more practical, safe, and beautiful *luminario*.

Directions

Collect several coffee cans; if you use various sizes, they will be easier to store by stacking one inside the other. Remove paper labels.

Fasten your wood in a vise, if one is available, so you can use it for support when punching holes in your cans.

Draw a star or other pattern on a heavy piece of paper and tape it to the can. See the star pattern on the next page; it can be enlarged on a copier to 150 percent. Put the can over the board for support and using a hammer and awl, or large nail, punch out the holes of your design. Do not try to punch directly over the board; set the point just beside the board in the vise so the awl can go through the can. Wiggle the awl and it will widen the hole a bit and come out of the can easily.

Make a holder for each light on your string from the wire by bending it in a tight loop twice around the plastic base of the bulb and bending it straight down, as shown in our diagram. You may need pliers to help you hold and bend the wire. Cut the wire three to five inches below the bottom of the bulb's base.

Arrange your lights along your front sidewalk, sticking the wire holder in the ground but leaving at least two inches between the ground and the bottom

Supplies needed

coffee cans

short piece of 2"x4" wood scrap

awl or large nail

hammer

string of large size Christmas lights, UL rated for outdoor use

moderately heavy wire or pliable wire coat hangers

pliers

wire cutters

vise, if available

of the base of the bulb. This way, your lights will be held up away from the dew or water that may be on the grass.

Cover your lights with your decorative tin *luminarios*, using the largest cans close to the house and graduating down to the smaller cans.

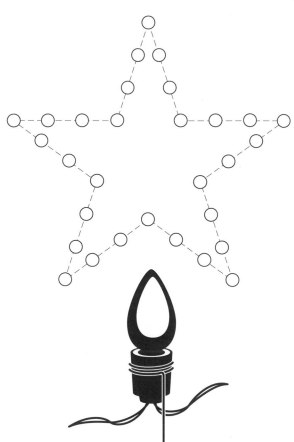

**Above, the finished *luminario.*
At left, the star pattern can be enlarged on a copier to 150 percent. The light bulb assembly is also shown.**

Chrismons

In the mid-1950s, Mrs. Harry W. Spencer, a member of the Lutheran Church of the Ascension in Danville, Virginia, created the first known Chrismons. The ornaments were created to "put Christ back in Christmas," and the original designs were patented worldwide in order to keep them out of the hands of the commercial world. Since that time, a number of churches and schools have developed their own Chrismon trees.

The term "Chrismon" comes from "Christ monograms." The ornament designs are copies of symbols carved or drawn by early Christians and found on old jewelry and on the walls of catacombs, buildings, and doorways in ancient Rome.

Early Christians often used signs, including many that were monograms for the name of Christ, to identify themselves and carry secret messages during times of persecution. Not just a Lutheran tradition, the Chrismons appeal to Catholics and Protestants alike.

The original Chrismons were made only in gold and white; later, silver was added in some places. White is the liturgical color for Christmas because it symbolizes our Lord's purity and perfection. Gold refers to his majesty and glory. Color, other than the tiniest touch, is not a part of these ornaments. Chrismons may be simple or elaborate. A simple set may be made of glittered satin balls or metallic pipe cleaners; more elaborate Chrismons may include fabric, lace, or beads. One woman used pearls from her daughter's wedding dress and gold braid from her mother's needlework to put family history into a Chrismon.

The Chrismons are not put on a regular Christmas tree, but hung on a tree of their own which is usually put up

Pipe cleaner Chrismons

for Advent. If lights are used, they should be plain clear bulbs, not colored.

A tree of this sort is an excellent Advent project for a Catholic school or CCD class and can be erected in the classroom, school office, or foyer of the church. The symbols for Christ serve as visible reminders of the One for whom the season is celebrated.

Choose one or more patterns from the Appendix, pages 157-59, to create your Chrismons, or research your own design.

Satin Ball Chrismons

Supplies needed

white satin Christmas balls

small piece of carbon paper

white craft-glue

toothpicks

gold glitter

waxed paper

small glass to prop ornament on

Christmas ornament hangers

patterns from the Appendix

Directions

Choose a design from the Christian symbols shown in the Appendix. Carefully trace the design onto the satin ball by putting a small piece of carbon paper between the design and the ball. Next, carefully trace over the design on the ball with white craft-glue, using a toothpick to apply the glue. Care must be taken to avoid runs; because the balls are round, the glue tends to run if it is not thick. For elaborate designs, you may need to glue and glitter one section in a first session and complete the design in a second session.

Working over a sheet of waxed paper, cover your glue design with gold glitter. Prop the ball on the top of a small glass to dry. When completely dry, shake off excess glitter and pour it back in the glitter container for reuse. Hang with an ornament holder.

Pipe Cleaner Chrismons

Supplies needed

gold or silver pipe cleaners

Christmas ornament hangers or thread for hanging

Directions

Choose a simple design such as the Chi Rho or the dove. Simply bend the pipe cleaners into the design chosen. You can enlarge the design to the size preferred and actually lay the pipe cleaner on the design to bend. Secure intersections by wrapping the cleaner around itself tightly. Hang with ornament hangers.

Why We Have Christmas Trees

The use of Christmas trees is a fairly recent custom in all countries except Germany, and even there it gained its popularity as recently as the end of the last century. The tree has its origin in a combination of two medieval religious symbols, the paradise tree and the Christmas light or candle.

About the eleventh century, religious plays were performed in or near churches. One of the most popular of the "mystery plays" was the paradise play, which told the story of creation and the expulsion of Adam and Eve from paradise after their sin. The play ended with a consoling promise of a coming savior, and was most popular at Advent. A fir tree hung with apples represented the garden of Eden and was the only prop on stage. The mystery plays were gradually forbidden in the fifteenth century because of abuses, but the people were so attached to the paradise tree that they began putting one up in their homes in honor of the feast day of Adam and Eve on December 24. Although the Latin Church never officially celebrated Adam and Eve as saints, the Eastern Churches did (and do) and their feast spread into Europe.

The paradise tree stood for the tree of life as well as the tree of sin; in addition to the apples representing the fruit of sin, the tree bore wafers representing the Holy Eucharist, the fruit of life. Later the wafers were replaced by candy and pastry representing the sweet fruit of Christ's redemption.

German cookie ornaments

In western Germany during the sixteenth century, the people began to transfer decorations from the Christmas pyramid, a form of candle holder, to the tree. Thus, glass balls, tinsel, and stars were added. During the seventeenth century the lights were added.

The Christmas tree arrived in America with the first wave of German immigrants about 1700. Its popularity today extends throughout the world.

Home-crafted ornaments can make your Christmas tree special. You can spend one or several pleasant evenings involving each member of the family in making beautiful handcrafted ornaments. Each ethnic group of Catholics has developed tree ornaments from its own heritage. We've given directions for several that you can make in multiples and personalize for your own tree or present to friends as small gifts.

Supplies needed:

Crayola Model Magic modeling compound

waxed paper

sharp knife

rolling pins

cookie stamps

markers

spray glue (or craft glue)

clear glitter

yellow ochre or light tan acrylic paint

brush

fabric paint in various colors

German Cookie Ornaments

Daughter Joanna brought me a number of cookies from Germany. One is a large, heart-shaped gingerbread cookie to hang on the wall; also, some small, stamped sugar cookies painted in bright colors and strung with ribbon. She bought the heart-shaped one at a fest, or celebration, she attended in Frankfurt. The small ones were purchased at a *Konditorei*, a type of German fancy bakery. Joanna said that she often saw children walking around wearing the cookies hung from a ribbon, worn like a necklace. At the *Konditorei*, some of the small cookies were sold as ornaments, although all were edible.

I asked Karin Murthough about this custom. She told me that fests, similar to our fairs, are popular in Germany. Some were held as marketplaces for local products; others were on holidays or feast days. All had a cookie booth. She says that when she and her brother attended one of the fests as children, their parents would always take them to the cookie booth and let them pick a favorite cookie. The cookies were usually decorated with words spelled out in sugar icing. The children wore the cookies proudly for the rest of the day. People would stop and look at the words on the cookies they had picked. She said they would keep their cookies a few days, much as we keep greeting cards, then throw them away. Karin's mother wouldn't let her eat her cookie for fear it would be "dirty," but Joanna said she saw a lot of the German children happily munching on their cookie necklaces.

We crafted our Christmas tree cookies out of modeling compound; we have too many insects in our Texas climate to hang real cookies on our tree.

German cookie ornaments

Directions

With a rolling pin, roll out the Model Magic onto waxed paper to a thickness of about ¼".

Using a sharp knife, cut your cookies into squares, or use a biscuit cutter to cut round ones.

Stamp your cookies with a cookie stamp. You can buy cookie stamps, or make your own. Or make a design by pressing the eraser end of a pencil and other "found" objects into the clay. (We give directions for making cookie stamps on page 118 of this book.) Punch a hole at the top of each cookie by cutting through the cookie with a plastic straw. Allow the cookies to dry overnight.

Decorate your cookies with markers. We highlighted the designs on the stamps and edged some with tiny dots. Spray with glue, or brush on craft glue mixed with a little water. Sprinkle with a tiny bit of clear glitter to simulate sugar.

Hang with a bit of curling ribbon or simply use a wire Christmas ornament hook.

Use a heart-shaped cookie cutter to make the gingerbread hearts. When dry, paint the cookies with yellow-ochre or light-tan paint mixed with water. Decorate with light-pink or white fabric paint to simulate icing.

Write German greetings in the center if you wish. *Oma's Liebling* (Grandma's Darling), *Mein Liebling* (My Darling), *Fröliche Weihnachten* (Merry Christmas), *Guten Tag* (Good Day), or *Ich Liebe Dich* (I love you) are all good choices. Make one with an extra-long ribbon for a favorite small child to wear as a necklace; just warn him not to eat it!

Ukrainian Straw Ornaments and Chains

The Ukraine, while under the reign of King Volodymyr (St. Vladimir), accepted Christianity from Byzantium in A.D. 988. Many pagan traditions in existence at that time were adapted by the Church to the new religion. Some have survived a thousand years and still form part of today's Ukraine Christmas celebrations.

As a part of the *Sviata Vechera*, or "Holy Supper," celebrated on Christmas eve, the head of a farming family brings in a sheaf of wheat called the "*didukh,*" which represents the importance of the ancient and rich wheat crops of the Ukraine, the staff of life through the centuries. *Didukh* means literally "grandfather spirit," so it symbolizes the family's ancestors. In city homes in Canada and America where so many Ukraine families now live, a few stalks of golden wheat in a vase are often used to decorate the table.

Although the custom of the Christmas tree did not have as early a beginning among Ukrainians, it has been a relatively common practice in Ukrainian household for many years. Evergreen trees are plentiful in the Ukraine, and Christmas decorations are made from materials found close at hand. Straw pieces are used frequently to fashion various ornaments. The Ukraine is famous for her wheat fields and has earned the name of "breadbasket of Europe." Both young and old enjoy using their creative talents in making intricate designs by joining short pieces of straw with small, brightly-colored glass beads on a heavy thread or fine wire.

In most parts of Canada and America, straw in its original form is not easily accessible, so commercial paper drinking straws are used with slightly larger beads.

Chains are common decorations. Shiny, colored paper is cut into various small shapes and joined through the center with pieces of straw and occasional beads to form chains. There are no definite patterns to be followed in these handmade objects — each one uses his own imagination to make the most attractive designs.

Ukrainian straw ornaments and chains

Directions

As mentioned above, there are no patterns; each person creates his own unique design. To form the ornaments, cut the straws into small, even pieces. 1½" or 2" pieces are a good length.

Thread your needle with nylon fish line. Slip on a bead and tie a knot to begin your ornament. Use a square knot and slightly burn the end of the line with a cigarette lighter to keep the knot from slipping loose. (An adult should help with this, if children are making the ornaments, or use cotton crochet thread if close adult supervision isn't possible.) Thread on a piece of straw and add another bead. You can resew through some of the beads to form three-dimensional designs.

To make the chains, cut 1" lengths of straws. Next cut small (½" to ¾" diameter) shapes from shiny paper such as the backs of old Christmas or

Supplies needed

spool of clear nylon fish line

large needle such as a darning needle

plastic drinking straws

pony beads

old Christmas cards or other shiny paper

other greeting cards. Since card backs are often only shiny on one side, you can fold one in half and paste it together with a glue stick before cutting.

Thread your needle with a long length of fishline and continue stringing pieces of straw, shiny paper, and an occasional bead in a pattern you like.

Note: Check your local office supply store. We found a hole punch that punches various shapes in paper made by Xonex Punch Art. We also found paper-cutting scissors by Fiskars that cut zigzag and scallop patterns.

Crochet-Edged Photo Ornaments

Needlecrafts have traditionally been used on decorations for American Christmas trees. A simple and very personal ornament can be made using single crochet and a favorite photo.

Directions

Cut basic geometric shapes (circles, squares, triangles, etc.) from colored card stock. Trim a favorite photo and paste it on the center of a shape. A 2-¾" diameter circle is about right for a school "wallet" type photo.

Write the name of the photo's subject and the year, or the words "Merry Christmas" and the year, on the back of your ornament with ball-point pen or marker.

Supplies needed

photos

scissors

glue stick

heavy white or colored paper (use colored card stock, not construction paper which fades)

laminating paper or clear Contac paper

scissors

hole punch

small crochet hook

shiny rayon crochet thread

small ribbon (optional)

Carefully laminate both sides of your ornament; trim laminating paper to the edge of ornament. If you like, you can laminate a small holy card or religious picture instead of the photograph.

Using a small hole-punch, make holes all around your ornament in an even line, with the top of the holes at least ¼" from the edge of the paper.

Slip the end of your thread through a hole at the top of your ornament. Hold the ornament between your left thumb and last two fingers and the thread between your first two fingers. Insert the crochet hook through the hole from the front to the back, catch the thread with the hook, and draw the thread through the hole toward you.

Now you have a loop over your hook. Use the hook to catch the thread and pull it through the first loop. Repeat this twice more until you have three stitches through the same hole. Now put your needle through the next hole over. Repeat the process and, in the same manner, work all the way around the outside of the ornament.

When you are back to the first hole, bring the loop through the hole but instead of bringing a loop through on the top, this time cut your thread about three inches from your hook and bring the end of the thread through the loop. Make a loop in this last piece of thread and tie a knot to hang your ornament.

You can finish by gluing a tiny bow at the top if you like.

Crochet-edged photo ornaments

Lacy Snowflakes

Tatting, an old lace-making art, has come down to us from the Middle Ages. In Italy, the art has a name meaning "eye," because of the similarity of the rings to the eyes; the French gave it a name to describe its delicate appearance; the Oriental name means "the shuttle." In America, we call it "tatting," probably from the word "tatters," as it is made in sections which are then connected. Our modern crochet also stems from this lace-maker's art.

Tatted and crocheted rounds make lovely and lightweight "snowflakes" for your Christmas tree. You can also cut lace medallions from scrap lace.

Supplies needed

medallions of lace, tatting, or crochet

liquid starch

waxed paper

bowl

Directions

Soak the medallion in the bowl of liquid starch until it has permeated all the fabric. Lay the wet medallion on waxed paper and put in the sun to dry. Carefully peel your "snowflake" from the waxed paper and hang on the tree. If you like, you can sprinkle on a tiny bit of iridescent glitter while the starch is wet, but they are beautiful just plain.

Why Do We Eat Mincemeat Pie at Christmas?

The traditional Christmas mincemeats pie comes from an old English custom. The British had various kinds of "minc'd pie" long before it became a Christmas custom. Crusaders returning from the Holy Land brought back all kinds of Oriental spices. The Feast of the Lord's Nativity began to be celebrated with a pie containing the rich spices of His native land.

Before the Reformation, mince pies were made in oblong form to represent the manger and honor the Saviour's humble birth. Sometimes a little figure of the child Jesus was placed on top of the pie. The pie was served as an object of devotion as well as part of the feast; the "baby" was removed and the children ate the "manger." The custom was suppressed by the Puritans in the seventeenth century and the pie was then made in a round, not oblong, shape to remove any trace of religious significance.

During the time of the Reformation, a number of writers of religious tracts called the pies "idolatrie in crust." As Alfred Cup Hottes reported in

1001 Christmas Facts and Fancies, one such writer said, "Such pye is an hodge-podge of superstition, Popery, the devil and all its works."

Elsie Sanford's potpourri pie can remind us of the Christmas mince pie as it brightens our home for the season.

Elsie's Potpourri Pie

Supplies needed

unbleached muslin

colored spray paint

white spray paint

inexpensive metal pie pan

potpourri

hot-glue gun and glue

white fabric-glue or craft-glue
  (optional)

iron

ground cinnamon or allspice

dried apple or orange slices
  (optional)

Directions

Spray the pie pan, inside and out, a color of your choice; blue or red is preferable. When the paint is dry, give the pan a quick, very light coat of white paint. Spray from a distance in order to make white flecks. You can spray a little white paint on an old toothbrush and flex it with your fingers to make a few tiny spots on your pan. Your inexpensive pan obtained from a dollar store or garage sale should now resemble one of the expensive enamelware pie pans.

Cut a strip from your muslin along the selvage edge that is 42" long by 4" wide. Make a fold along the entire length of the cut edge that is ½" wide. Double the fold over a second time to form a stiff edge. Iron the fold in place.

With the folded edge lined up along the outer rim of the tin and the selvage edge toward the center, use a hot-glue gun to place spots of glue approximately ¾" apart along the rim, gluing the fluted crust in place; use a clothespin to press the fabric into the glue until it sets (a few seconds) and letting the fabric fold up between glue spots to form flutes. The clothespin keeps your fingers from getting burned and makes a nice flat bond.

Continue fluting and gluing around the rim; lap the edge over slightly and cut off excess. When rim is completely fluted, go back and glue the selvage inside pan.

Cut six strips of fabric 12"x2½". Fold in ½" and double over until your strip is between ½" and ¾"glue in width and stiff. Iron strips flat.

You can use a thin line of white craft-glue or fabric-glue to keep the strip from unfolding if you like. Attach the ends of three of your strips with the fold side toward the bottom of the pan to the edge of the tin, approximately 1¼" apart. Attach three more strips in the same manner along the inside edge of the second quadrant of your pie. Crisscross the strips to form the top lattice of the pie as shown in the diagram.

Elsie's potpourri pie

Stuff your pie with potpourri, heaping it slightly above the top of the tin. You can purchase pretty blends of potpourri or make your own from our recipes found on pages 129-31.

Glue the lattice strips inside the edge of the tin. If you like, glue a dried apple or orange slice to the center of the top of your pie. Sprinkle the pie with ground cinnamon or allspice to simulate a real pie.

Display your pie on the dining room table or kitchen counter, or seal in a gallon size zipper bag if you are planning on giving it as a gift.

When your pie begins to loose its fragrance, you can resurrect it by sprinkling a few drops of potpourri oil directly on the potpourri (be careful not to get any on the fabric lattice or edge). Seal the pie in a zipper bag and let it stand for a few days before displaying again.

Why We Give Gifts at Christmas

The practice of giving presents stems from an old Roman custom called "*strenae*" (lucky omens). On New Year's Day, the people of ancient Rome exchanged gifts as tokens of their good wishes for a happy year. At the advent of Christianity, like so many other pagan customs, the gift-giving custom was adapted, spread, and became a part of the actual Christmas celebration. Christians presented gifts to their friends at Christmas in honor of the baby Jesus.

In Germany, the packages of Christmas gifts presented to children were called "Christ bundles." Another way of presenting gifts in Germany, and later in England, was the "Christmas ship," in which bundles for the children were stored. Special carols for the occasion were sung in both countries.

In medieval times in Britain, the priests emptied the alms boxes in all churches on the day after Christmas and distributed the gifts to the poor. In imitation of this practice, many people of the working class kept their own personal boxes of earthenware and stored their savings there all year. At Christmas they received the last flood of coins from patrons, customers, and friends. The day after Christmas, they broke the boxes and counted the money. Eventually this custom of giving and accepting presents became known as "boxing," and the 26th of December is known as "Boxing Day" in Britain.

A similar custom grew up in Holland and some parts of Germany, where the children were taught to save their pennies in a pig-shaped earthenware box. Throughout Europe, the pig was a symbol of good luck. The children could not open the pig until Christmas, so it was called the "feast pig." A remnant of this custom remains in our piggy banks of today.

Christmas gift giving in America is a combination of two old European customs: the gift giving of St. Nicholas, who left small gifts in stockings on the eve of his feast, and the gifts the children found under the tree on Christmas day, which they believed were brought by the Christ Child.

In most European countries, the Child Jesus was the gift bringer. He came with angels during the night to decorate the tree and leave presents for the children of the household. In Spanish-speaking countries, a crib scene was set up with an empty manger. The Christ Child brought gifts for the children and his image was found in the manger on Christmas morning. In Italy, Lady Befana, a sort of fairy queen, brings the children's presents on January 6, Epiphany. In Russia, a legendary old grandmother named Babushka is the gift bringer. The legend is that when the Magi were on the way to Bethlehem, Babushka misdirected them on purpose, delaying their visit to the baby king. She repented, and on Christmas eve goes about looking for the Christ Child and taking gifts to all the children in His name.

"Christkindl" is the diminutive name of the Christ Child, the gift-bringer in Germany. The custom came to America with the German immigrants in the middle of the last century, but Christkindl was gradually adapted in the form of Kris Kringle, or Santa Claus.

Saint Nicholas was one of the major, most popular, and beloved saints of pre-Reformation Europe. The celebration of his feast, including his gift bringing, had spread to most parts of Europe. After the reformation, many countries abolished his feast and forbade veneration of the saint. A Christmas Man was substituted for the saint, and soon the cult of Saint Nicholas was forgotten in many countries.

The memory of St. Nicholas was impossible to obliterate in Holland because for centuries this nation of seafarers had venerated him as the patron of their ships. A statue of the saint was often the figurehead on the prow of Dutch boats. When the Calvinists tried to eradicate the saint and substitute the Nordic Christmas Man, they succeeded only in obliterating the religious details of his past. Sinter Klaus, dressed in his bishop's garments, still arrives mounted on a white charger to visit little children on the eve of his feast.

Sinter Klaus emigrated to America with the Dutch settlers and continued to visit the children, filling their wooden clogs with his presents. After British settlers founded New York, they found the kindly bishop more appealing than their own Father Christmas, especially because the bishop brought gifts for the children.

The Dutch pronunciation of his name became Americanized to Santa Claus; he lost his bishop's robes and donned the secular dress of Father Christmas, although he kept his original colors. His visit was transferred from December 6 to Christmas Eve, and he acquired his home and work factory at the North Pole, his sleigh, reindeer, and the custom of sliding down the chimney from the Christmas Man. He retained the practice of placing his gifts in the children's shoes or stockings.

In the nineteenth century, the Christmas custom of Santa Claus spread throughout the United States. As the country grew more prosperous and more secular, the presents at Christmas grew more expensive and elaborate. Today, clever merchandising beginning at Thanksgiving has obscured much of the holy and religious significance of Christmas. The holiday hysteria has so pervaded the season that many non-Christians have adapted their own religious celebrations at this time of year and have adopted the custom of Santa Claus and his gift giving. Customs which crossed the ocean to our shores have been altered and, by the middle of this century, were returned to

Europe in their altered form, changing the face of the celebrations they initially stemmed from.

All the original Christian gift-giving customs denoted good will on the Christ Child's birthday. Perhaps it is time to take a long look at the Catholic heritage of our Christmas customs and return some of their initial simplicity and religious significance.

Stamp-of-Approval Bookmark

Supplies needed

used stamps

colored paper or brown paper bag

pen

glue stick

scissors (pinking shears, too, if you have them)

laminating paper or clear Contac paper

Directions

Check your mail at home and at work; save envelopes with pretty or unusual stamps.

Cut two strips of colored paper, making one slightly smaller than the other. 8"x2" is a good size for a bookmark. Construction paper works, but fades rapidly. Colored typing paper is nicer. Or try strips cut from a brown grocery bag and plain white typing paper.

The larger strip should have straight edges; the smaller can be pinked if you like. Paste the strips together with a glue stick.

Cut the stamps from the envelopes, leaving a little of the envelope as backing; pinking really looks nice. Arrange the stamps in a pleasing pattern and paste them to the front of your bookmark; write a personal message on the back.

Cut your laminating paper at least ½" wider and longer than your marker. Carefully laminate both sides of the marker. Using a coin, press down the edges carefully. Then cut off the excess. Laminating is tricky! Carefully read the instructions that come with the laminating paper to avoid wrinkles.

If you like, finish by punching a hole and tying a ribbon at the top.

Stamp-of-approval bookmark

Photo Earrings

Directions

Cut 2 strips of silver paper from the back of an old Christmas card 2½" long and 7/8" wide. Thread paper clip through loop at bottom of ear wire.

Fold a strip of silver paper exactly in half and crease bottom. Carefully put glue inside the fold and glue the paper to the paper clip as shown in the diagram. Hold the paper together tightly with your fingers until the glue holds.

Cut a special person's photo into a circle or oval. Cut a second photo exactly the same size as the first. Put a drop of glue on the back of the photo and attach to the front side of your silver paper "frame."

If you wish, you can finish by adding a tiny ribbon bow at the top of each earring.

Supplies needed
1 pair fish hook ear wires
2 standard paper clips
heavy silver paper from back of an old Christmas card
craft glue
photo with heads approximately ½" in diameter
tiny ribbon bows (optional)

Photo earrings

Christmas Card Sachets

When my mother passed away a few years ago, we found a little box of paper Christmas sachets that had never been opened in a long-forgotten corner of the Christmas decoration storage area. From the price and the design on them, we inferred they had probably been made in the 1950s. How surprised we were to open the box and discover the sachets still retained a faint but pleasant smell!

The sachets were stamped on the back "handmade original." Naturally, nosy old me took one apart to see how it was done. I was surprised to find them filled only with a small square of corrugated cardboard.

This is a good way to recycle those beautiful Christmas and other greeting cards you haven't the heart to throw away. One or a few would be a perfect little token gift for neighbors or teachers. Take a handful to distribute the next time you visit the hospital or nursing home. Or use them yourself to impart a pleasant scent to your closets and drawers. Their low cost makes this a perfect class project.

These probably will not retain their scent for over forty years (remember, Mama's were closed tightly in a box), but the addition of the orris root will cause the pleasant smell to linger for a long time.

Supplies needed

scissors

corrugated cardboard

old greeting cards

essential oil

powdered orris root

plastic zipper bags

white craft-glue and clothespins

or

hot-glue gun

coffee can or large jar with
   wide mouth and lid

tweezers (optional)

Directions

If you want all of your sachets to be the same size, you can take our pattern at right (page 33) and draw around it on the top side of the card, attempting to center the square over the main part of the design. This will work but unfortunately will result in some patterns overlapping to the back, and it will be difficult to find parts of the design exactly the right size.

If you don't have enough cards but want to use the idea with a class, you can draw a design for the center of our pattern and use it as a master copy to Xerox onto pretty paper instead of using the cards. Paper a little heavier than typing paper works best.

Children can decorate the sachets in a number of ways before cutting and gluing. For example, if your design was a simple Valentine heart copied on red paper, the children could decorate it with a white paint pen before finishing their sachets.

Our alternative method will result in sachets of varying sizes, but the design on the front of the sachets may be more pleasing.

Select a card with an interesting part of the design somewhere near the center. Cut off and discard (or save for other projects) the back of the card.

Make the envelope, using the folding instructions on page 34.

1. Bend the card backwards along an imaginary straight line at the top of the part of the design you have chosen. Next, bend it backwards along an imaginary straight line at the bottom. The two flaps bent backwards must overlap by at least ½"; if the lap-over is more than this, the excess can be cut off.

Unfold the card and repeat the process on each side, making folds where

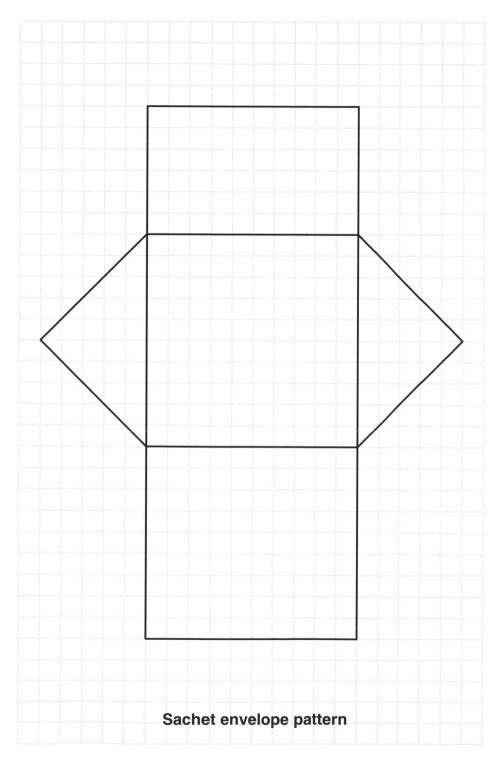

Sachet envelope pattern

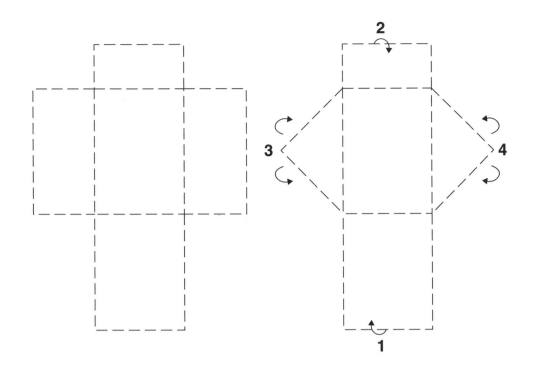

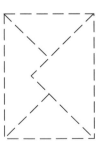

How to fold the sachet envelope

you want the side of the design to be. Again, the flaps should overlap. Unfold the card.

2. From the sides, make four cuts along the top and bottom folds, cutting only to the side scores. Cut down from the top and up from the bottom along the side scores until you reach the top and bottom folds.

3. If one flap is excessively long, cut off the excess.

4. Starting at the corners of the frame, make slanted cuts to form two triangular flaps on opposing sides. Leave the other pair of flaps as rectangles.

5. Your sachet "envelope" is now ready to fill, fold, and glue. Repeat this process to make as many envelopes as you wish to make into sachets.

Make the center filling: If you are making the sachets as a class project, the teacher should make all the centers for younger children. They may be pre-made and stored in a plastic zipper bag. Older children can do this part but need to be cautioned not to get any of the orris root or the oils near their eyes or mouth. Orris root isn't deadly poison, but ingestion can make you very sick. Some essential oils are strong enough to burn.

Using a knife or case cutter, cut small squares of corrugated cardboard for the center part of your sachets. These do not need to exactly fill the inside of the sachet; they can be somewhat smaller. Squares that are 1"-to-1½" square are a good, workable size.

To add the scent, work over waxed or other heavy paper to avoid getting any of the oil on furniture. It can ruin the finish on wood.

You will need a clean coffee can or jar for each type of oil you use. We suggest you stick to only one or two types. One of the stronger oils such as patchouli or lavender is probably best. Both have the additional benefit of repelling insects. You can, of course, mix the oils, but that type of experimentation is not appropriate for a class project.

Place a few drops of the essential oil in the center of each piece of corrugated cardboard. When all are oiled, place them in a clean coffee can or large jar. Add approximately 1 teaspoon orris root for each 5 centers. Shake well to distribute the orris root across the oily part of the cardboard. Remove the centers and lay them out to dry for a few minutes on a piece of waxed paper.

Put it together: Using a pair of tweezers, carefully lay a center inside one of your envelopes. You can use your fingers, but this gets messy and you need to remember not to taste! Fold over the square flaps first. Put a dot of glue on each triangular flap, and fold over one at a time. It is best to use white craft-glue for this, especially when working with a class group. If so, use a clothespin to hold the flaps in place until the glue dries. If you are in a hurry, use your hot-glue gun.

Store your completed sachets in plastic zipper bags. Do not mix two different scents in the same bag. You can leave them in the bag when giving them as gifts to make the fragrance last longer. A lapidary shop will usually have smaller plastic zipper bags for sale, and one major manufacturer has recently come out with a snack-size bag that is a good size for this. Present your sachets in an attractive card if you like.

Christmas card sachets

The Easter Season

Carnival

Strings of multicolored beads and gold doubloons fly through the air as gaily decorated floats wend their way through the streets of New Orleans, Galveston, and a number of other cities throughout the United States. Fantastically garbed and masked revelers celebrate riotously at Mardi Gras — the carnival which marks the approach of Lent. Feasting and reveling, all the familiar features of our modern carnival celebrations are firmly rooted in a tradition that actually dates from about the 14th century.

The main reason for carnival celebrations is to feast and rejoice before the imminent season of fast and abstinence. The intensity of our human nature to anticipate approaching privations by great excesses should not be judged by the mild Lenten laws of today, but by the strict and harsh observance of ancient times. The good people of past centuries felt entitled to have a good time before they started on their awesome fast.

In ancient times, the law of abstinence was much stricter and included many other kinds of food besides meat. People began abstaining progressively during the pre-Lenten season until they entered the complete fast on Ash Wednesday. The name carnival comes from the Latin *carnem levare* (*carnelevarium*), which means "withdrawal" or "removal" of meat. The German word for this time of carnival is *Fassnacht*, or *Fasching*, which probably comes from the ancient "*vasen*" — a word which means "running around crazily."

The feasting at carnival stems from a practical reason — the necessity of finishing those foods which could not be eaten during Lent: meat, butter, cheese, milk, eggs, fats, and bacon. The week before Ash Wednesday, there was an increased consumption of rich foods and pastries. From this, we get the names "Fat Tuesday" (*Fetter Dienstag* in German; *Mardi Gras* in French), "Butter Week" (*Sedmica syrnaja* in Russia and the Slavic countries), and "Fat Days" (*Tluste Dni* in Poland.)

As a time of feasting, carnival celebrations the world over developed many traditional foods for the celebration. England enjoyed her famous Shrove Tuesday pancakes and dollops of sliced meat mixed with eggs and fried in butter. *Fastelavnsboller*, muffins filled with whipped cream and coated with frosting, were traditional in Norway; Russians served rich, unsweetened buckwheat pancakes known as *blinni*. The Scots ate *crowdie*, a kind of porridge cooked with butter and milk. Germans baked pastries called *Fassnachtstollen*. In New Orleans and Galveston, a special cake known as a king's cake is baked and served at parties. The guest who receives the slice containing a tiny figure of a baby (perhaps Baby Jesus) is the one who will host the party the following year.

Many elements of the Indo-European, pre-Christian spring lore have traditionally been included in carnival celebrations. Our pre-Christian ancestors had many rites and celebrations to drive away winter and welcome the fertility of spring. Lent excluded the boisterous practices of mumming and masquerading, so what better time for these than the gay days of carnival? The mummer's parade in Philadelphia stemmed from this tradition. In pre-communist days in the country regions of Russia, a fantastic figure called *Masslianitsa* was gaily decorated and driven about on a sledge while the peasants sang special songs. At the end of the week, this butter goddess was burned and a formal farewell was bidden to pleasure until Easter.

In Latin countries, much of the pre-Christian element of the carnival frolics seem to have stemmed from the celebration of the Roman *Saturnalia*, a pagan feast in honor of the field god Saturnus which was annually held in December. Our pre-Christian ancestors knew nothing of biology, but through observation knew of the life that sprang from eggs. One of the best-loved Latin traditions of fiestas and carnivals are the *cascarones*. These are eggshells filled with confetti. Laughing party-goers crack the shells over one another's heads for good luck. In the southwestern United States, these *cascarones* have become a traditional feature not only of the pre-Lent carnivals but also at Easter and fall celebrations.

The popes acknowledged the carnival practice in Rome and tried to regulate its observance, correct its abuses, and provide entertainment for the masses. In 1471, Paul II started the famous horse races which gave the name *Corso* to one of Rome's ancient streets. He also introduced carnival pageants for which the Holy City was famous.

In the centuries following, other cities developed special features of their carnival celebrations, such as the parade of gondolas in Venice, floats and parades in South America, and carnival balls in many cities throughout Europe.

The two best-known celebrations of carnival in the United States today are the Mardi Gras celebrations held in New Orleans and Galveston. The celebrations in both cities are hallmarked by the selection of a king and queen, a parade, and the large Mardi Gras costume balls, both public and private. Some of today's balls are held as fund-raisers for charity; many private parties are just for fun. Crewes, or groups of participants, have special coins minted and these, along with the traditional strings of brightly-colored beads, are thrown to the crowds as the parade passes by. Participants are encouraged to wear fancy dress, and items such as gaily feathered masks and silvery, ribbon-decorated coronas are popular items sold by street vendors along with plenty of food and beer. Bands from throughout both states travel to the cities to play in competition. Thoroughfares are thronged with crowds, all happily celebrating the last fling before the coming somber period of Lent.

In many countries, such great excesses were committed at carnival that the bishops sought to prepare the people for the penitential season by exposing the Blessed Sacrament solemnly in the churches for forty hours in memory of the time during which the Sacred Body of Jesus was in the sepulchre. Pope Benedict XIV, in 1748, instituted this special devotion for the three days preceding Lent, calling it "Forty Hours of Carnival." The devotion was at one time held in many churches of Europe and America in places where the carnival frolics were of general and long-standing tradition, and was a precursor to today's Forty Hours Devotion.

Cascarones

Traditional in all Latin countries, *cascarones*, or confetti-filled eggs, are used at carnival and fiestas. Amid much laughter, people break the eggs over each other's heads to wish the recipient good luck. A bowl

Cascarones

of the gaily decorated *cascarones* makes a sparkling centerpiece for the carnival table.

Supplies needed

1 small box cellulose wallpaper paste (obtain from your local paint or wallpaper store)

confetti

clean, empty ("blown") eggshells

colored tissue paper

egg dye or food colors (optional)

glitter (optional)

bottles, small glasses, or empty egg tray to perch eggs on while they dry

Directions

First, cover your work surface with waxed paper to protect your table or counter and prevent eggs from sticking. Using a large darning needle or an ice-pick, make a small hole in one end of each egg and a larger hole at the other end. Blow the contents of the egg into a clean bowl. The eggs can be scrambled or used for baking. Rinse the shells carefully and allow to dry. If you like, color the eggs with egg dye or food colors and again allow them to dry.

Tear colored tissue into small pieces. Mix up a small bowl of the wallpaper paste according to package directions. Spoon confetti into the shells until they are about 1/3 to 1/2 full. Dip a piece of the tissue into the paste and carefully cover the hole to prevent the confetti from spilling out. Add several more pieces of colored tissue to add color to the *cascarone*. Sprinkle on a little glitter or confetti to make them more festive. Perch the completed egg on the mouth of a bottle, small glass, or an egg carton turned upside down, until completely dry, then pack in egg cartons until time for use.

Carnival Crown and Mask, or Door Wreath

Glittery crowns and gaily decorated crowns and domino masks are sold by vendors at every corner during Mardi Gras for revelers who don't come equipped with their own costume. Make our simple, but effective, mask and crown to wear yourself, to sell at school carnivals, or put them together for an attractive seasonal door or wall wreath.

Directions

For mask: Bend pipe cleaner in half and twist center tightly for 1". Wrap ends tightly around a pencil to form spirals, and bend outward slightly. Glue the twisted part of pipe cleaner at the center top of mask to form antennae. Cut 2 feet of curling ribbon in a contrasting color. Holding ribbon tightly against the blunt edge of a scissors, between scissors blade and thumb, pull ribbon to form curls. Glue a curly strip across top of mask using several small dots of hot glue. Let ribbon dip down and attach at beginning of antenna near the nose. Hint: Use a chopstick or pencil to press ribbon onto hot glue to avoid burning fingers. If you like, add three silver foil stars at random on mask.

For crown: Cut 2 yards of the silver star garland. Twist the garland into a circle approximately 7" in diameter for adult size; 5" to 6" is child size. Cut 9 or 10 strips of curling ribbon in various lengths from 1½ to 3 yards long. We chose red and white to go with a red metallic mask. Center the ribbon at one spot in back of crown and tie tightly. Curl each strip by passing the ribbon across the blunt edge of a scissors, pressing tightly with your thumb as above. If you like, add a few silver or foil stars along the ribbon or at ends. You will need to use 2 stars in every place you want a star, sandwiching the ribbon between the stars or else the sticky back of the star will stick in places you don't want it to.

Supplies needed
1 domino mask (obtain at party shop, or buy at Halloween and save for the carnival season)
1 silver pipe cleaner
2 yards silver star garland (obtain at card shop, dollar store, or buy at Christmas and save)
2 or more colors of thin paper curling ribbon
hot-glue gun
silver and colored foil stars (optional)

Carnival mask

For wreath: Cut rubber band holder off of mask. Attach mask to crown diagonally across from ribbon and at a slant. This wreath is so light you can hang it on the wall or door with a regular dressmaker or push pin.

Hint: The metallic garlands now come in a variety of colors and have hearts for Valentine's day, shamrocks for St. Patrick's day, etc. These simple crowns can be used as favors for a little girl's birthday party, or to crown a king or queen of almost any holiday. If you want to celebrate carnival and Mardi Gras beads and doubloons aren't easily available in your area, obtain lengths of plastic beads on a string from your fabric store or use leftover Christmas bead garlands. Cut to a length that can be easily slipped over your head. Attach the ends with a hot-glue gun, or carefully burn the end bead with a cigarette lighter and push it against the other end bead to join. Simulate doubloons with foil-wrapped "coins" from the local candy store.

Lent
Stations of the Cross

The Stations of the Cross are 14 tableaux which depict 14 important events in the Passion and death of Our Lord. The stations are the prevailing popular devotion in Lent, and both the Eastern and Western Church practice them. The devotion originated at the time of the Crusades when the knights and pilgrims began to follow the route of Christ's way to Calvary in prayerful meditation, according to the ancient practice of pilgrims. The devotion spread throughout Europe and developed into its present form through the efforts of the Franciscan friars in the 14th and 15th centuries.

Although the devotion was in existence from apostolic times, it was in later years that the stations became similar to the devotion as we know it today. The Franciscans, determined to bring the sacred places of Palestine to the world, began promoting the devotion in the 15th century.

Throughout the years, various names have been given to this devotion: Way of the Cross, *Via Dolorosa*, Stations of the Cross, and Way of Christ's Sorrows. An Englishman named Wey was the first to use the word "stations" to describe the 14 halts in the procession following along the Way of the Cross. These halts were made for meditation and prayer, and each commemorated some specific incident on the road to Christ's sacrifice. The number of incidents commemorated varied from five to 14. Originally, the stations were made in inverse order, beginning at the garden of the tomb and finishing in the judgement hall of the Praetorium. St. Leonard systematized and arranged the stations according to the actual sequence of events.

Many beautiful meditations have been written for this devotion and there are meditations using scriptures, those written especially for children, those which reflect modern problems, and short meditations for use in the missions. Many of today's meditations add a 15th station in honor of the Resurrection. Traditionally, in making the stations, one moves from one spot to another while meditating on the passion of Christ.

Our Stations of the Cross are made to be nailed along a fence line so that the maker can move from one station to another. These could also line a hallway in a house, or be fastened to stakes or laid along a garden path to allow for private meditation. Any out-of-the-way or private place will do. We used only the patterns, but you can use the electric engraver to add the number of the station or write out the description of each station if you choose.

Outdoor Metal Stations of the Cross
Directions

Turn a gold-colored square of aluminum on a slant so that the square becomes a diamond. Place a piece of carbon paper between one of the patterns (found in the Appendix, pages 160-62) and the aluminum and trace the design with a ball point pen.

Using the electric engraver, go over all the lines of the pattern. If you like, put a Roman numeral at the bottom of the diamond to indicate which station the design represents.

Supplies needed
electric engraver
14, 4"x4" gold-colored aluminum squares
1, 6"x6" gold-colored aluminum square
carbon paper
hammer and small nails
protective eyewear
patterns from the Appendix

Complete all fourteen of the stations. The last pattern represents the Resurrection and should be centered on the 6"x6" square. Nail the stations along a fence.

Hints: The aluminum squares for this project can be obtained at your local trophy shop or hardware store. From the trophy shop, these are used as plates for the bottom of trophies and are gold colored; the writing shows up as silver. If you can only find the silver-colored ones from the hardware store, darken the lines by spraying the design with black enamel paint and quickly wiping off the paint from the face of the square, leaving the black paint only in the lines.

When using the electric engraver, write as if you were using a pencil, but hold the engraver straight up. Write very slowly. You may find it helpful to obtain a piece of scrap aluminum and practice before attempting the project. Always use safety glasses, as the engraver can cause small chips of metal to fly off the plate; these chips could lodge in your eye and cause severe problems.

Palm Sunday
Palm Crosses

Our pre-Christian ancestors had a number of fertility rites they celebrated in spring. One of these was the touch with the "rod of life." Any maiden hit with the branches broken from a young bush was believed to obtain the blessings of health and fertility. The custom became popular all over Europe, and during carnival or Eastertide girls and women were tapped with leafed rods or pussy willow branches that were often decorated with flowers and ribbons. A relic of this tradition remains today in the modern practice of throwing the bridal bouquet at weddings. The ancient symbolism is revealed by the claim that the girl who catches the bouquet will be the next to marry.

In medieval times, the greater part of the pre-Christian usage and meaning of the rod of life was transferred to the Christian symbolism of the palms which the church blesses on Palm Sunday.

From the time the Church obtained her freedom in the fourth century, the faithful in Jerusalem reenacted the solemn entry of Christ into the city by holding a procession in which they carried branches and sang the "Hosanna." In the early Latin Church, the people at Mass on this Sunday would hold aloft twigs of olives.

The solemn blessing of these "palms" seems to have originated in the Frankish kingdom about the beginning of the eighth century. By medieval times, the custom of a procession on this day had spread throughout Europe. Our Lord was represented by the carrying of the Blessed Sacrament or by a crucifix adorned with flowers. Later, the people began to draw a wooden statue of Christ sitting on a donkey in the center of the procession. These *palmesel* (palm donkeys) are still seen in some of the museums of Europe. By the end of the middle ages, the processions became restricted to circling the church. The procession wound through the churchyard where the outdoor crucifix was covered with flowers and the people knelt at the graves of relatives and prayed while the priest sprinkled the graves with holy water. Although today's ceremonies are usually performed completely within the church, the custom of visiting the cemeteries on Palm Sunday is retained in some places.

Throughout the world, there are a number of different names for the Sunday before Easter that stem from the type of plants used. Until recent years, in most parts of Europe real palms were unavailable so other branches were used and gave their names to the Sunday. Olive branches were used in Italy; spruce, willows, pussy willows, box, and yew were common in Ireland, England, and Germany.

Centuries ago it was common to bless various flowers of the season as well as the "palms." The day became known as "Flower Sunday" in a number of countries: Blossom or Flowering Sunday in England, *Blumensonntag* in Germany, *Pascua Florida* in Spain, *Pâsques Fleuris* in France, *Cvetna* in the Slavic nations, and *Zaghkasart* in Armenia. The term *"Pascua Florida"* originally meant just Palm Sunday, but it was later applied to the whole festive season. When Ponce de León first sighted the land on March 27, 1513, he named our own state of Florida in honor of the great feast.

It became customary in many places to take the blessed palm received on Palm Sunday home and place it behind the crucifix or over a door to be saved as a sacramental throughout the year with a prayer for blessing of the home. An old Czech custom was to burn part of the palm during a storm to avert disaster. In earlier days, many parishioners returned the palm to the priest the following year and these were burned to provide the ashes for Ash Wednesday. This is done even today in some parishes. Persons who had no crucifix often folded the palm into a small cross.

A small cross made of blessed palms and decorated with flowers is simple to make. A good group project would be to ask the priest for leftover palms, make them into these crosses, and take them to shut-ins or residents of nursing homes on Easter. They are light enough to be pinned to the wall with a pin and serve as a lovely reminder of the Easter season throughout the year.

Directions

As palms begin to dry out, their edges curl. Grasp the palm tightly between your thumb and fingers and slide it through them to uncurl the edges of the palm. If the palm is too dried to flatten out in this manner, soak it in a bucket of very hot water for about 20 or 30 minutes.

Hint: if you have to soak the palms, let them

> **Supplies needed**
> blessed palms
> small dried rosebuds or other dried flowers and leaves
> hot-glue gun or white glue
> stapler
> potpourri oil (optional)

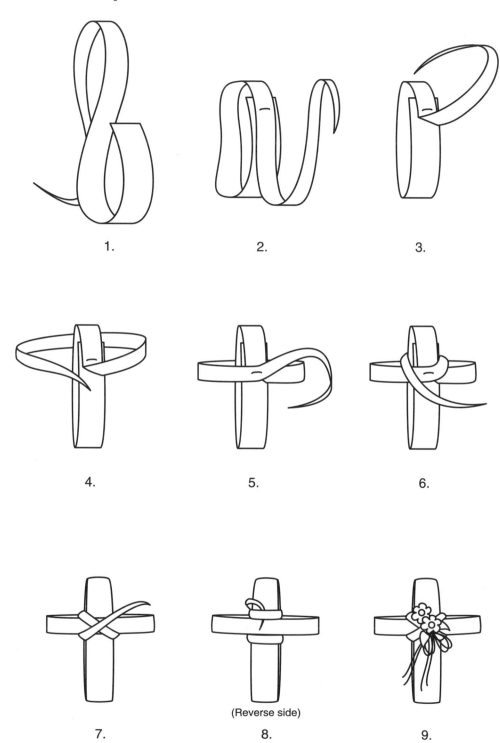

1.

2.

3.

4.

5.

6.

7.

8.

(Reverse side)

9.

dry for a day before attempting to glue on the flowers.

Blessed palms are generally about 22" or 23" long; measurements here are approximate so you will have to use your judgement as to the length of each loop. (See diagram on page 46.)

1. Holding the palm strip with the curled edge toward you, fold up the widest end in a loop about 2" long.

2. Then fold the top piece downward until it covers the top of the previous fold and forms a loop about 2" long. Place a staple at the intersection of the loops.

Above, unfinished crosses; at right, the finished product

3. Bend the palm to the right, creasing on a diagonal line.

4. Fold the palm behind the cross, forming a loop about 1½" on the right side.

5. Continue the fold toward the front of the cross forming a loop 1½" on the left. Secure in the center with another staple.

6. Wrap the remainder of the palm over the top right angle of the cross, bringing it straight across the back and over the top left angle to the front. Cross it diagonally to the bottom right corner . . .

7. . . . straight across the back and bring it to the front from the bottom left corner. Bring it from the bottom left corner to the top right corner and to the back again.

8. Weave the small remaining piece in the back under the loops and tie it off. If needed, you can use a third staple or drop of glue.

Glue a tiny arrangement of flowers in the center of the cross. If you wish, you can add a tiny bow. If you are using dried flowers obtained from a craft shop, you may wish to use a toothpick to add a drop or two of potpourri oil to the cross. Hung on the wall in a sickroom or nursing home room, or over a door in your home, the gentle odor of the potpourri will sweep across the room each time the door is opened for several weeks.

Hint: For a single cross or two, pick dried flowers from a bowl of potpourri you may already have on hand; for a group project, purchase the dried flowers in bulk from a craft shop.

The Cross — *In Hoc Signo, Vinces*

Supplies needed

1 cup flour

½ cup salt

water

knife

cookie cutter

straw

gold spray paint

clear acrylic spray

acrylic paints

"jewels"

ribbon

clear glitter

white glue

food colors

waxed paper

foil

When Constantine won the Battle of Milvian Bridge in 312, he attributed his victory to the Christian God. On the afternoon before the battle, he told of seeing a luminous cross in the sky with the words, "In this sign, conquer." On the following night, Christ appeared to him in a vision and invited him to have a standard made in the form of a cross. From then on, the Emperor's armies bore this triumphant standard, and the Christian church emerged from the catacombs as the persecutions were ended.

The cross is the most widespread and venerated sacramental of the Church. This symbol of mankind's redemption has been used since the early days of the Church, and today it is present in all Catholic and most Christian churches.

During the early church persecutions, the cross was often disguised as a part of other symbols such as an anchor, or hidden in a monogram. Until the end of the sixth century, they were shown without the figure of the Redeemer. The usual crucifix seen today first gained popularity in the 13th century.

Through the centuries, crosses have been made worldwide and celebrated with artworks in many distinct forms.

Bread-Dough Crosses

An inexpensive clay made in your own kitchen can be used to make a variety of crosses.

Basic Clay and Working Tips

In a medium mixing bowl, mix 1 cup flour and ½ cup salt. Gradually add up to ½ cup water, stirring until mixture forms a ball. Turn dough out onto a floured surface and knead for 7 to 10 minutes, until smooth and elastic. Use the dough as you would clay.

Roll dough out on a floured surface to ¼" thickness and cut or stamp design with a sharp knife or cookie cutter. To attach two pieces of dough, moisten with water and pinch. All shapes should be less than ½" thick for best results.

Make neat holes for hanging by punching a soda straw into the clay before baking. Transfer your project to a cookie sheet covered with foil and bake in a slow oven,

A variety of crosses

300°, about 30 minutes for medium-sized pieces, or until they turn a light golden brown. When cool, place your project on a wire rack and let dry overnight before decorating. Unused clay can be stored in an airtight plastic bag for a few days. After painting, and before decorating with faux jewels, spray with several coats of clear acrylic spray to seal the project.

Antique Jeweled Cross

Cut a paper pattern for a plain cross 3½" long by 2" wide. The width of the stem is ⅝" and the crossbar is ½". Lay pattern on clay rolled to ¼" and carefully cut around the pattern with a small sharp knife. A small hole for hanging is made with a toothpick. Seven holes lengthwise and five holes crosswise are made by punching the dough with a soda straw. When cross is baked and thoroughly dry, spray with gold paint. Finish by setting faux jewels in holes and attaching with white glue. Our jewels came from a box of broken beads, but they can be purchased at a craft or fabric store. The family button box is also often a storehouse for "jewels."

Medieval Braided Cross

Dough is cut into narrow strips ¼" by 10" for the stem and 6" long for the crossbar. Three strips are braided in a simple braid and the ends are pinched into a rounded shape to finish. Moisten the braids in the center to attach the crossbar. The hole for hanging is made with a soda straw. The heart is cut with a cookie cutter and holes are punched around the edge with a straw to make indentations to set the pearls. Moisten the center of the braids to attach the heart. When cross is baked and dry, spray with gold paint and set pearls with white glue.

Stone Chi Rho *Cross*

Mold dough into a cross with rounded tips, 5" long with a 4" crossbar. If dough is slightly thicker than ¼" it will usually bake unevenly, giving a good surface texture to the cross. Use a thin straw or a toothpick to form a hole for hanging. When our cross was baked and dried, we sprayed it with Flec It, a special paint that gives a granite-like texture to the project. The paint is available in most hobby shops and some paint stores. Or paint the cross a stone gray or brown with acrylic paints. Then add flecks of color by rubbing your finger across the bristles of an old toothbrush dipped in paint. This is messy, so put paper around the surrounding area thoroughly before beginning. The *Chi Rho* symbol (see Appendix, figure 1, page 157) was painted with white acrylic paint. A final coat of clear spray finishes the project.

Sugar Cookie Kitchen Cross

Cut a paper pattern for a cross 9" long with a 5" crossbar. The four tips of the cross flare out slightly. Place pattern on dough rolled to ¼" and cut with a sharp knife. We used a cookie stamp to make a raised pattern of hearts and flowers and highlighted the design with acrylic paint. You can experiment with different objects to create a design; if you don't like your design, re-roll the dough and begin again. Or simply paint on a small, intricate design.

Spray the finished cross with clear spray and sprinkle on clear glitter while the spray is wet for a sugar-frosted effect.

Spanish Mission Cross With "Glass" Insets

Our mission cross measures 9"x5", and was cut from a paper pattern on ¼" dough. A straw is used to punch the hole for hanging. Pastry cutters are used to make round holes on the bars and a pointed cutout in the middle. When the cross is baked and dry, glue small pieces of foil over the cutout designs from the back, pushing with fingers to make a leak-proof backing. In a paper cup, mix approximately ¼ cup white glue with 3 to 5 drops of red cake color. Stir to mix thoroughly. Place cross on a flat surface, foil side down. Pour the glue mix into the holes. It will take 24 to 48 hours for the glue to dry, depending on the thickness you poured. When completely dry, the glue mix will be transparent and glossy. Carefully remove foil with a sharp knife. Finish painting the cross with acrylic colors.

Valentine Cross

We used a 3"x3" heart shape cookie cutter to press out the basic shape of our Valentine cross from dough rolled to ¼". A small, plain cross is cut freehand from the center of the heart. Baked and dried, the Valentine cross was sprayed with gold paint. An 8" piece of red florists' ribbon was looped through a curtain rod ring and hot-glued to form a hanger. The heart was attached to the ribbon with hot glue.

Hint: Remember to seal the back side of crosses for permanence.

Salvadoran Wooden Cross

The artisans of La Palma, El Salvador, have a unique and joyful way of depicting the relationship between spiritual and secular aspects of life. Traditional wood

Salvadoran wooden cross

Supplies needed

6" piece of 1"x2" board

11½" piece of 1"x2" board*

gesso

paintbrush

sandpaper (optional)

colored permanent markers

fine-point black permanent marker

clear acrylic spray

white paint

white glue

hammer and 2, 1"-long nails

small picture hanger or drill

carbon paper

objects such as crosses and angels are decorated in bright, clear colors with motifs that often include the houses of the villages and the local flora and fauna. The bright colors, simple drawings, and high gloss finish give their art a unique style.

Our Salvadoran-style wooden cross is simple and inexpensive enough to make as a group project. Follow our design, or create your own.

Directions

Nail the crossbar of the cross to the upright, 2½" from the top. Put a spot of white glue between the two boards before nailing for extra strength. Drill a hole or attach a small picture hanger to the back for hanging.

Paint the cross with gesso. Remember to cover your work area, as gesso hardens like plaster and is difficult to remove. Wash brushes thoroughly and immediately if you plan to reuse them.

Let dry, sand rough spots, and paint with a second coat of gesso. Paint the cross white. You can use white spray paint, acrylic paint, or interior wall paint. Using carbon paper, carefully trace the patterns at right on your cross. (The pattern can be enlarged or reduced in size on a copier, depending on the size of your cross.)

With colored markers, color the designs. Use the brightest colors. You can use acrylic paints if you don't have markers. Then go over the outline of the designs with the fine-line black marker.

Allow to dry thoroughly. Before you spray your project with clear finish, read the section on spray painting on page 13. If this part is not done correctly, you will ruin your project.

Finish your cross with several coats of clear spray to give it a high gloss finish and bring out the color.

Hint: If you make our miniature Czech-style home altar on page 62 from a grape crate, you will have as leftover pieces of wood two pieces of 1"x2" exactly the right size for this project.

This design can be enlarged or reduced on a copier, depending on the size of your cross

Hint: For your clear spray, use a high-gloss acrylic spray. Other types may turn your whites yellow. The first coats must be especially light or your colors will bleed. It is a good plan to finish a scrap of wood and spray paint it to see if you have the technique.

Easter Eggs

The custom of decorating special Easter eggs developed among the nations of northern Europe and Christian Asia soon after their conversion to Christianity. Their history stems from the fertility lore of the Indo-Europeans.

Our pre-Christian ancestors knew nothing of science and biology, and were startled to see a live creature emerge from a seemingly dead object — the egg. Thus, the egg became a symbol of spring and fertility. Converts to Christianity gave the egg a religious interpretation, seeing it as a symbol of the rock tomb out of which Christ emerged to new life.

Eggs were one of the foods forbidden during the long, harsh fast of Lent, and they became a special sign of Easter joy. The faithful painted and colored eggs in gay colors. Then they had them blessed and ate them or presented them as gifts to friends.

During medieval times, eggs were traditionally given at Easter to all servants and to the children along with other gifts. In most countries, the eggs were dyed with simple vegetable colors. The Chaldeans, Syrians, and Greeks dyed the eggs crimson in honor of the blood of Christ. The Slavic countries made their distinctive *krasanki* and the masterpieces of patient labor called *pysanki*. The Armenians decorated blown egg shells with religious pictures as gifts, and in part of Germany the eggs were decorated and hung from shrubs and trees much like a Christmas tree. The use of sugar to form Easter decorations became popular in southern Germany at the beginning of the last century.

During the last years of Tsarist rule in pre-revolutionary Russia, the royal family commissioned many works from the talented jeweler Peter Carl Fabergé. Among these were a number of beautiful Easter eggs crafted by the master jeweler and his artisans from precious metals, jewels, semiprecious stones, and exquisite enamel work. In his own private Russian revolution, Fabergé insisted that the value in an object lay not in the value of its components but rather in its craftsmanship and design.

The exquisite Easter eggs were gifts exchanged by the Tsar and Tsarina at Easter. Most of the eggs contained a "surprise" inside; others had mechanical works. The first Imperial Easter egg was presented to the Empress Maria Feodorovna in 1884. The pleasure the egg gave both the Tsar, who presented it, and the Tsarina, who received it, caused them to establish a custom which continued without interruption until the violent end of the Romanov dynasty.

Sugar Eggs

You can craft a baker's dozen of our sparkling sugar Easter eggs in the style of Fabergé to present as special tokens of Easter joy to friends or to decorate your Easter table. Later, the "surprises" in or on them can be removed and they can be eaten or used to sweeten a pot of tea.

Directions

In a large jar or container with a tight lid, place 3 cups granulated sugar, 15-20 drops of lemon or other edible essential oil (use less if you choose peppermint oil), and ¼ cup water. Shake vigorously until the water is distributed throughout the sugar. Pour the sugar into a bowl.

With your fingers, pack the sugar firmly into the halves of a plastic Easter egg. Immediately turn the molded sugar out onto a waxed paper covered smooth surface. This part of the project is similar to the way children mold sand castles at the beach. Leave the egg halves to dry overnight, or speed up the drying time by placing them on a cookie sheet in a low (300°) oven with an open door for an hour or so. (Any eggs broken can be crumbled up, put back in the jar with a drop or two of water, shaken, and remolded. Leftover flavored sugar can be used to sweeten a special glass or cup of tea.)

When the eggs are hardened enough to handle, use a small spoon such as a grapefruit spoon to scoop the sugar out of some of the egg halves to make peek-a-boo eggs.

Place 1 cup powdered confectioners sugar in a cup and add 3 teaspoons water. Stir until you have a thick paste, which will be your glue. Put a blob

Supplies needed

3 cups granulated sugar

I cup powdered sugar

lemon or other edible essential oil (optional)

water

cake colors

Cake Mate snowflake decors

toothpicks

found objects such as tiny figurines, a crucifix, etc.

small plastic Easter egg mold (we used a leftover from last Easter and the container from Silly Putty)

of this glue on one half of an egg. Attach the other half of the egg by pushing it slightly in a circular motion against the half with the glue. Finish gluing all the egg halves together, except any that you want to make scenes inside of, and set aside to dry. Use your fingers and some of your glue to fill in any gaps in the edges of the join.

You can make a peek-a-boo egg by hollowing out the halves and making a small round hole in one end of the egg. Arrange a little scene inside the egg before gluing the halves together. The angel egg used one half hollowed-out and glued to the top of the other half, which was laid face down. A lamb and an angel came from a miniature manger scene left over from Christmas.

The crucifix egg uses a silver crucifix glued with sugar glue to the flat half of an egg. Circle the crucifix with a string of plastic pearls. Tiny silver candy beads could also be used for this special egg, which is perfect for presenting to a new catechumen during the Easter season.

The ribbon, leaves, and colors on the flower eggs were made by coloring a small amount of the sugar glue with cake colors. Put a small amount of the glue on waxed paper or a jar lid. Add a drop of cake color and stir with a toothpick. Use the toothpick to apply the color to the egg. Flowers are Cake Mate candy snowflake decors.

Hints: Look all over the house for small items that might make miniature decorations for your eggs. Check the baking section of the local grocery store for cake decorations that will spark up your eggs. Plastic pearls are available by the foot from the fabric store.

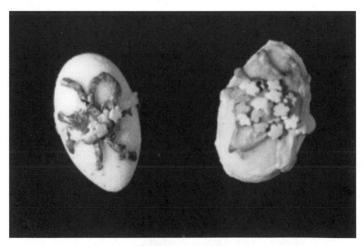

Sugar eggs

January and February

January 1 — New Year's Day
Greek House Blessing Hanging

Joanna's travels in Europe and the Orient have added greatly to my own home decor; she has brought back works of art from all the countries she has visited. Knowing that I have a passion for religious art, she has searched out different religious items as presents for me. One of the most unusual is a beautiful brass and glass Greek amulet containing an icon portrait of Our Lady and a large eye. She noticed these amulets hanging on or by the door of many of the Greek houses. When she asked about them, she was told they were a symbol of a blessing on the house, and used to keep away evil.

Insofar as the efficacy of such a charm is attributed to anything other than the power of God, such amulets would, of course, be superstition and forbidden to Catholics. Used as a sacramental, or symbol for the blessings and power of God, however, these can be good reminders of our faith. We made ours of modeling compound and painted it to resemble metal, and used symbols to indicate the power of God.

Directions

Using a rolling pin, roll out clay on waxed paper to ¼" thickness. Using a hole punch, punch a hole in the top center of the holy card, about ¼" from the edge of the card. Place the laminated card on top of the clay and use a sharp knife to cut the clay around edge of card to form back of frame. Roll out two long, thin (about ⅛") "snakes" of clay long enough to encircle frame. Twist the snakes together to form a rope and circle the card,

Supplies needed

Crayola Model Magic
  modeling compound

laminated holy card of Our
  Lady of Perpetual Help

metallic gold or bronze acrylic
  paint

paint brush

waxed paper

sharp knife

rolling pin

hole punch

white satin cord

1 gold or white curtain rod ring

pressing the clay to the back to form a frame for the picture. Stick the point of a pencil through the hole you punched in the card to make a hole in the clay backing.

From another segment of the rolled-out clay, cut an equilateral triangle with the sides about 3" long. Cut an eye shape and center in the triangle. Cut a small circle about ¾" in diameter for the iris of the eye and lay on top of the eye shape. Score a circle inside this circle to give the impression of a pupil. Line the bottom of the eye with a single thin clay "snake." Line the top of the eye with a rope made of two thin "snakes" and twisted together. Punch a hole at the top of the triangle with a soda straw.

Cut a letter "A," or alpha, from the rolled-out clay. The legs of the "A" should be about 2½" long. Pull a piece of the clay at the top up and punch a hole with a straw. Roll a long "snake" and use it to form the omega symbol (see the diagram in the Appendix, figure 12, page 159), laying it on top of the alpha to form the Greek alpha and omega symbol. Allow your pieces to dry overnight. Turn the picture with the back to the air to allow for thorough drying.

Greek house blessing

Using gold or bronze acrylic paint, paint all the pieces. Let dry.

Take the satin cord and fold it, letting one end be about 6" longer than the other. Pass the looped end through the hole in the picture so it's about 3" long. Tie twice. Then tie the longer end of the cord to the hole at the top of the alpha and omega symbol. Use a square knot. Tie the shorter end of the cord to the hole in the top of the Eye of God and secure with a square knot, so the eye hangs about halfway between the alpha and omega symbol and the bottom of the picture frame.

Leave as is, or add a little Byzantine glamor by gluing on faux jewels or use fabric paint to highlight the haloes.

Ask your priest to bless your hanging as a sacramental so it becomes a reminder of the power of God and the perpetual help that Our Lady stands ready to give you, instead of a superstitious amulet. Hang your blessing beside the door of your home.

January 6 — Epiphany

Holy water is ordinary water sanctified by the blessing of the Church. In the Roman ritual, the priest prays, "May this creature of yours, when used in your mysteries and endowed with your grace, serve to cast out demons and to banish disease. May everything that this water sprinkles in the homes and gatherings of the faithful be delivered from all that is unclean and hurtful; let no breath of contagion hover there, no taint of corruption; let all the wiles of the lurking enemy come to nothing. By the sprinkling of this water may everything opposed to the safety and peace of the occupants of these homes be banished, so that in calling on your holy name they may know the well-being they desire and be protected from every peril through Christ our Lord. Amen." A special blessing of water on the Eve of the Epiphany was approved for the Roman ritual in 1890. This blessing comes from the Orient, where the church has long emphasized the mystery of our Lord's baptism in her celebration of Epiphany. Water blessed during the Easter Vigil is known as Easter Water.

The blessing of this water reminds us of Christ, the living water, and of the sacrament of baptism, in which we were born of water and the Holy Spirit. Whenever we are sprinkled with this holy water or use it in blessing ourselves on entering the church or at home, we thank God for his priceless gift to us and we ask for his help to keep us faithful to the sacrament we have received in faith. Christ's faithful are permitted to take holy water home with them to sprinkle the sick, their homes, farm fields, etc. It is recommended that they place it in fonts in their homes and use it to bless themselves frequently.

Holy Water Bottle

Directions

Save a colored glass bottle such as cough syrup comes in. Wash clean and dry. With a wax pencil, write the words "Holy Water" on it, then draw a simple Christian symbol such as a cross. Always use protective eyewear when engraving

Supplies needed

electric engraver

wax pencil

colored glass bottle with lid

protective eyewear

on glass; without protection, small glass chips can fly up and get in your eye!

Using the electric engraver, write slowly and carefully over the wax design. The engraver should be held in your hand, as you would a pencil, except nearly perpendicular to the working surface. Write slowly, using small strokes.

When you are finished, wash the glass dust off your design. The design will show up as a white line, so the darker the bottle, the better. Use your bottle to obtain blessed holy water from your church.

Potato Print Valentine Cards

Our American custom of sending Valentine cards came from England. The traditional

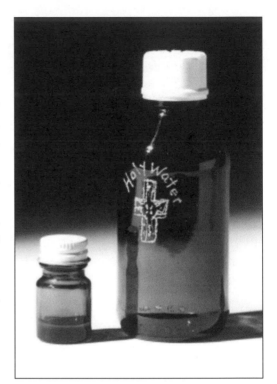

Holy water bottle

words actually imply: "You are my Valentine, and I offer you my companionship, affection, and love for the next twelve months and am willing to consider marriage if this companionship proves satisfactory for both of us."

The Duke of Orléans is believed to have made the first Valentine card while imprisoned in the Tower of London in 1415. He wrote love poems to his wife in France. Sweethearts exchanged handmade cards in some places during the 17th and 18th centuries. In France, these were huge paper hearts trimmed with yards of real lace.

In the United States, Valentine cards became popular during the Civil War. Elaborate cards trimmed with spun glass, satin ribbons, and sometimes mother-of-pearl ornaments were sold. For a time, Valentine's Day was as big an event as Christmas.

We used a potato to print handmade Valentine cards.

Directions

Cut a potato in half as evenly as possible. Potato printing works best with blocky designs; cut with a thin, sharp blade.

On one half of your potato, sketch a simple heart shape. Carefully run your knife blade around the outside of your design. Cut away the part of the potato you *don't* want to print. Your design should stand up in at least ¼" relief. You can leave your heart solid, or cut out the middle. On the other half of your potato, cut a leaf shape.

Supplies needed

potato

small-bladed, sharp knife

tempera paint

brush

thin line marker

bottle of iridescent fabric paint — optional

pack of blank cards and envelopes

Before printing, stamp your potato a few times on newspaper to remove some of the liquid. Brush tempera paint on the raised portion of your potato and stamp on cards.

When you have completed stamping your cards, you can add stems to the heart "flower" and leaves. We made hot pink hearts with bright green leaves and blue stems.

With a thin marker, add the stems and any words or greeting you like.

When your card is dry, you can highlight your design with glittery fabric marker if you wish.

Potato print Valentine cards

March

March 19 — St. Joseph's Day
Czech-Style Miniature Home Altar

Home altars have been popular in many countries in styles ranging from a simple table holding a Bible and a candle to an elaborate carved shelf holding a statue and flowers. Many Czech and Bohemian homes contained elaborate home altars that simulated a small church. This custom crossed the ocean, and even today some of these altars can be seen in areas where descendents of the original immigrants settled. The ones I have seen were hand-made of wood, painted white and gilded on the carved pieces. They were usually quite large, about two or three feet in width and height. Placed atop a bureau in a bedroom, or in the family room, the altars held statues of favorite saints, flowers, relics, and often included photos of deceased family members.

Few of today's homes have room for such a large altar. You can easily make a miniature altar that can sit on a shelf or hang on a wall. These are particularly nice for a child's room, as children are especially drawn to visual reminders. We used ours to display a 7" statue of St. Joseph, to whom we owe so much.

Directions

Carefully remove all nails from the crate. Save all wood for other projects. One of the end pieces of the crate will become the main part of your altar. The end of a grape crate is a 13"x5½" rectangle with the corners cut off. (See the diagram on the facing page.) Draw a line across the rectangle 4" from the bottom

---

Supplies needed

grape crate (obtained from the produce department of your local grocery store)

l pair chopsticks

saw

wooden beads

hammer & small nails

star anise (from spice department of the grocery store)

gesso

paintbrush

white paint

gold paint

picture hanger (optional)

glue gun and hot glue and/or white glue

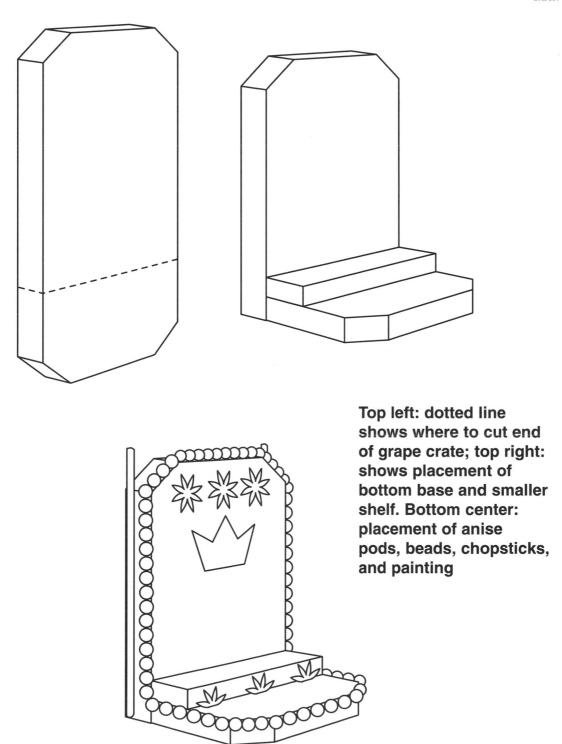

Top left: dotted line shows where to cut end of grape crate; top right: shows placement of bottom base and smaller shelf. Bottom center: placement of anise pods, beads, chopsticks, and painting

and carefully cut along the line with a saw. An electric saw is nice, but a small hand or coping saw will do. The 4" piece will form the bottom of the altar; the 11" piece will be the back.

Stand the 11" wood piece on the 4" piece to form a right angle and nail the pieces together with at least three nails. Put a line of white glue along the edge before nailing.

The feet of a grape crate are made of 1"x2" lumber. Saw a piece 5½" long from one of the feet. Glue and nail this piece to form a step at the base of your altar. This shelf does not have to butt up to the back part of your altar; it can sit a little forward if the base of your statue is wider than the width of your 1"x2" shelf.

If you plan to hang your altar on the wall instead of setting it on a shelf or dresser, attach a picture hanger to the back at this point.

To further decorate your home altar, glue the two chopsticks, pointed ends down, along the sides of your altar's back. Thread wooden beads on small nails and nail them to the top of the altar back. Using a glue gun, glue a string of inexpensive wooden beads completely around the outside edge of the back and base of your altar.

Glue several star anise pods across the top of the back and along the edge of the shelf. Follow our diagram, or make your own pattern. If you cannot locate star anise, you can make your design with small wooden beads or whole cloves.

Spread paper generously over your work area before you begin to gesso your altar, because gesso hardens like plaster and is difficult to remove. Coat the entire altar, including the beads and anise, with gesso. (Wash the brush thoroughly and immediately if you plan to re-use it.)

Let dry, sand rough spots if you

Czech-style home altar, shown with a statue of Mary

wish, and add a second coat of gesso. Allow to dry overnight. Paint the entire altar white. You can use a glossy spray paint, acrylic paint, or a semi-gloss paint that you would use on the interior walls of your house. When the paint is thoroughly dry, highlight the beads and the anise with gold paint. If you like, you can paint a gold crown shape behind the head of your statue. Complete your altar by making miniature vases from perfume bottle caps and add tiny dried or artificial flowers for color.

May

Why Is May Mary's Month?

"Oh, Mary, we crown thee with blossoms today, Queen of the Angels, Queen of the May." Many American Catholics remember the beautiful May crowning ceremonies of a few years ago: girls dressed in frothy white dresses and boys with slicked-down hair and grown-up ties processed with songs, rosary beads, and a floral crown to place on the parish statue of the Virgin.

Today, a number of parishes and schools across the nation are reinstituting this beautiful custom. Along with their human mothers, they again honor their heavenly mother. May is traditionally held to be the month of Our Lady. But why? Although May is a contraction of the name Mary, the month was probably named for Maia Majesta, the Roman goddess of grain. The people of ancient Rome celebrated the first day of May by honoring Flora, the goddess of flowers. She was represented by a small statue wreathed in garlands, and a procession of singers and dancers carried the statue past a sacred, blossom-decked tree. Later, festivals of this kind spread to other parts of Europe, reaching their height of popularity in England during the Middle Ages. Dances around a flower-bedecked May pole were common, and the festivities often blossomed into riotous and wild occasions. Often a May queen was chosen as part of the festivities.

Devotions to Our Lady on the first days of May date from medieval times, when St. Philip Neri (16th century) began the custom of decorating the statue of the Virgin with spring flowers. Annibale Dionisi, an Italian Jesuit, proposed devotions to Mary throughout the entire month. Just as happened with other pre-Christian customs and festivals, the Church incorporated the May celebrations and gave them a Christian dimension. May began to be celebrated in honor of Our Lady with much the same type of festivities, including floral tributes and processions.

You can honor Our Lady during her month by making a May crown for your home statue.

May Crown

Directions

Decide which statue you will crown. If you have a picture instead of a statue, make the crown in the same manner, but drape it over the picture instead of tying it as a crown.

Make small, tissue-paper flowers following the directions on pages 124-25 of this book, adjusting the pattern to a size that will be appropriate for your statue or picture.

the directions on pages 124-25 of this book

Cut a strip of florist's ribbon long enough to go around the head of your statue and tie, leaving streamers hanging down the back. Starting at the center of the ribbon, glue on flowers to circle the head of your statue. When dry, tie on the crown and cut streamers to an appropriate length.

Supplies needed
blue or white florists' ribbon
white craft-glue or glue gun
tissue paper flowers

Mother's Day

Mother's Day was first observed in Philadelphia in 1908. In 1914, President Woodrow Wilson proclaimed the second Sunday in May as a time for public observance of Mother's Day. Children honor their mothers on this day with gifts, visits, and flowers. Traditionally, the wearing of a colored flower by a child signifies a living mother; a white flower is worn in memory of a deceased parent.

Father's Day was first celebrated in Spokane, Washington, in 1910, and in 1924 President Calvin Coolidge proclaimed the third Sunday in June as the celebration for fathers.

Today's custom of Mothers' and Fathers' Days has spread from America throughout the world. We are not, however, the country of origin for similar celebrations.

In the English Church, the 4th Sunday of Lent was known as Mothering Sunday. In times past, children took offerings to the church in which they were baptized and then visited their parents, usually bringing a present. A simnel cake, a type of rich plum cake, was one of the traditional gifts.

In Spain, December 8, the feast of the Immaculate Conception, is kept as a sort of Mothers' Day. The great feast of Our Lady has also become an outstanding day of joyful family celebrations in honor of mothers everywhere in the country.

Silhouettes

In colonial days, the paper-cutter, or silhouette, artist was in great demand for making profile likenesses. His art was a thriving business in an age when costly oil paintings were the only alternative if one wanted a portrait made. Besides those who made a living by cutting pictures, there were thousands who cut paper for pleasure.

In Europe, the few people who went into silhouette cutting as a fine art perfected their craft and some of their cuttings stand out as true art. In America, the art took on a pioneer vigor, well-seasoned with Yankee humor, and flourished with true democracy; as a hobby, it was adopted by those in all walks of life.

The name "silhouette" first appeared in 1798 and was used to describe the cut-paper profiles which were the hobby of an unpopular French finance minister, Etienne de Silhouette. The craft itself, however, has its origins in classical antiquity and according to Pliny (A.D. 24-79) was called "skiagraphia," made by tracing the outline of a shadow cast upon a wall. Silhouettes of hands in red pigment go back to Palaeolithic times and are found on pottery as early as the second millennium B.C.

As an art, silhouette cutting belongs to a select few "born artists." As a craft, however, we can have endless fun with this simple and inexpensive hobby.

In the field of religious art, Sister Mary Jean Dorcy, O.P., was known worldwide for her beautiful paper cuttings. Dan Paulos, whom she personally encouraged, is also renowned for his beautiful paper cuttings of the Virgin. His fragile silhouettes of the Virgin and Child have made him known around the world as a religious artist. His art reflects his deep faith. He says, "I love what I do because every day is a prayer. Each piece of art involves meditation and concentration. My whole life at home is a prayer; I'm thanking God constantly."

For many years, my mother taught first grade. One of the nicest Mothers' Day gifts she had her

Supplies needed

a copier with the capability to reduce originals

large piece of white paper

geometric-patterned wrapping paper

brightly-colored paper (not construction paper; it fades)

photo mat

sharp scissors

glue stick

pencil

lamp

masking tape

students help to prepare was a silhouette of themselves, cut from black paper and framed. We've updated the idea using brightly-colored paper.

Directions

Set up the lamp to shine on a wall. Tape a large piece of paper to the wall with masking tape at approximately the height the shadow of the child's head hits the wall.

Stand the child between the lamp and the paper to cast a good shadow. Turn the child's head until a good silhouette is cast.

Tell the child to stand perfectly still (young children can't do this for long, so you have to work rapidly!).

Silhouettes

Trace the child's silhouette onto the paper with the pencil. Try to trace details such as eyelashes and cowlicks.

Take down the paper and draw over your lines to darken them.

Reduce your silhouettes to the size you prefer on a copy machine that has reducing capability. If you don't have one available at work or home, take your silhouettes to a local office supply store or your nearby library. If needed, you can fold your paper and reduce it half at a time; simply tape the two halves back together. (You can, of course, use them full size, but this makes quite a large picture.) You may want to reduce your silhouettes to two different sizes; one to frame and another to decorate the front of a Mothers' Day card. We made one set about 7" tall and the other about 5".

Carefully cut around your reproduction with very sharp scissors to make a pattern. You can curve the neck to simulate a shirt or other attractive neckline. Embroidery scissors or straight-blade nail scissors work well. Trace your pattern onto colored paper. Construction paper will fade, so choose a high quality of paper, such as origami paper. Use a glue stick to paste your silhouette onto wrapping paper with a geometric design. Frame it with a photographic mat. You can also frame your silhouette in an inexpensive picture frame.

An attractive card can be made by folding an 8½"x11" sheet of paper in half. Paste a smaller rectangle of wrapping paper to the front of your card and paste the silhouette on top of that.

Box of Love

For Mother's Day or any day, make a box of love.

Supplies needed

12" of ⅛"-wide ribbon

1" square box (a small cardboard box such as jewelry comes in will do)

small piece of wrapping paper

small card and pen

Directions

Wrap the tiny box as a present. Tie a ribbon bow. Print the following poem on a small card:

This is a very special gift
That you can never see.
The reason it's so special is
It's just for you from me!
Whenever you are lonely
Or even feeling blue,
You only have to hold this gift
And know I think of you!
You never can unwrap it,
Please leave the ribbon tied.
Just hold the box close to your heart.
It's filled with LOVE inside!

Feast of the Sacred Heart (Friday of the second week after Pentecost)

The Sacred Heart of Jesus symbolizes God's love for us in a humanly concrete and profoundly attractive way. The devotion began about the 12th century and became increasingly popular in the 17th century after the visions of St. Margaret Mary Alacoque at Paray-le-Monial. In 1899, Pope Leo XIII consecrated the whole world to the Sacred Heart of Jesus.

Sister Julia Madeleine Sophie Hurley, R.S.C.J., designed a three-dimensional emblem of the Sacred Heart. Cut from lightweight paper and sewed with thread, the emblem can hang in a window, over a desk, or from a piece of wood stuck in a bottle. Each slight puff of wind twirls the emblem merrily. A number of the colorful little emblems were hung on branches as decorations and favors at Sister Julia's diamond jubilee as a Religious of the Sacred Heart.

Sacred Heart Emblem

Directions

Fold two pieces of colored paper and cut out the pattern as shown in the diagram on the following page. Place the two emblems together, then sew up the middle, beginning at the bottom of the heart, leaving enough thread to hang your emblem. Crease the folds so the heart has a 3-D effect.

Supplies needed

light-weight colored paper

scissors

needle and thread

Box of love

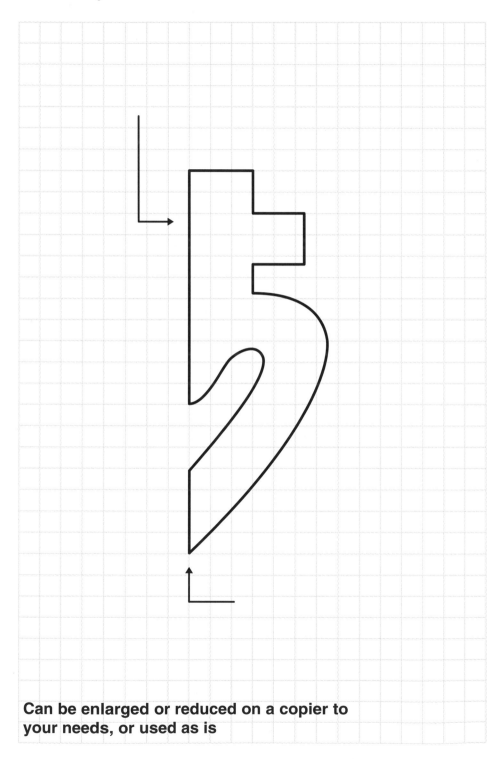

Can be enlarged or reduced on a copier to your needs, or used as is

June, July, and August

June 13 — St. Anthony of Padua

For centuries, there has been a shrine in honor of St. Anthony of Padua in the mountainside village of Lach, Albania. Through the centuries, the shrine has drawn pilgrims from throughout the country. A two-mile-long steep and rocky trail, dubbed "the pilgrim's road," leads to the shrine; its rugged surface underscores the penitential aspect of pilgrimages to the shrine.

On the way to the shrine, pilgrims stop to carve a cross into one of the stones that mark the borders of the trail. Each pilgrim carries a walking stick which he has made himself. A cross is carved into the top of each staff to remind the pilgrims that they are walking with Christ. Early Franciscans in their missionary journeys through the country began this tradition of using walking staffs emblazoned with the cross. On arrival at the shrine, the pilgrims present hand-carved crucifixes to be blessed. After Mass and special devotions to St. Anthony, the pilgrims break their two-day fast and share a picnic of bread, cheese, onions, and desserts.

The blessed crucifixes are taken home and hung over the bed of the sick person for whom the pilgrimage has been made. If the person is cured, the pilgrim will make a return visit in order to hang money on the trees around the shrine. They feel that in this manner, people in need will receive the help of St. Anthony. On the saint's feast, as many as 50,000 pilgrims usually visit.

During the Communist era (1944-1990), all pilgrimages were banned, but the people ignored the prohibition. At first, the Communists blew up the shrine with dynamite, but the people continued to come. At last, powerless in the face of the faith of the sturdy Albanian Catholics, the Communists contented themselves with sending organized squads to pick up the money for their "cultural" activities.

With Albania's return to freedom, the shrine at Lach is again the site of organized pilgrimages, and the Albanian Franciscans are in the process of restoring the shrine, which had been totally destroyed by the despots but never forgotten by the faithful.

In Siauliai, Lithuania, there is a Hill of Crosses. Pilgrims bring handmade crosses and place them there, indicative of the constant trials and tribulations of the Lithuanian nation, as well as its Christian hope for a better tomorrow. This particular Hill of Crosses was visited by Pope John Paul II in 1993, and he too placed a cross there with the following inscription: "Thank you, dear Lithuanians, for this Hill of Crosses, bearing witness to the European nations as well as all of the nations of the world as to the great faith of this nation."

Albanian Walking Staff

With the popularity of walking as a form of exercise, a lightweight staff is useful to carry with you. It can help you navigate steep areas or protect against challenging animals. The cross can remind you, as it does the Albanian pilgrims, that you are walking with Christ. A quiet morning walk is definitely a good time for mental prayer. If you aren't a walker, hammer a large nail securely into the bottom end of the stick. Use bolt cutters or heavy wire cutters to cut off the nail head and use your stick as a handy tool to help you pick up pieces of trash paper in your yard without the necessity of bending over.

Supplies needed

long wooden handle (use an old broom, or purchase a new replacement handle at a discount store)

saw

acrylic paints and brush

masking tape

fine line black permanent marker or paint pen

clear acrylic spray

pattern in the Appendix

Directions

If you use an old broom, cut off the bristle part and wash to remove dirt. Cut your staff to the length that is most comfortable for you.

The traditional colors are red, yellow, and green, but unless you're using an old broomstick that is very worn, any color will do. The Albanians carved the cross at the top of their staffs, but unless you have wood carving tools and skill in this craft, you can draw your cross about ½" to 1" from the top with permanent black marker or a paint pen. The cross with the double-headed eagle is an Albanian symbol and might be a good choice.

You can add bands of color by wrapping a piece of masking tape around the handle and wrapping a second piece about an inch below the first. Paint around the handle between the tapes. Let the paint dry between stripes. When you remove the tape, you will have nice straight edges on your lines. You can paint on one or more of the other Albanian symbols shown on page 178.

When your designs have dried, spray a light coat of clear spray over them to keep them from rubbing off so easily.

July 14 — Blessed Kateri Tekakwitha

In 1980, Pope John Paul II beatified the American Indian maiden, Kateri Tekakwitha, in a beautiful and moving ceremony attended by over four hundred of her fellow Native Americans.

Blessed Kateri was born in 1656 at what is now Auriesville, New York, and baptized into the Catholic faith in 1676 near Fonda, New York. She died at Caughnawaga, Canada, in 1680. This young Indian virgin took as her maxim in life to search in all things for what would be most pleasing to God.

Silent and prayerful, Kateri was persecuted by her relatives, who resented her forsaking their ancestral beliefs. She escaped to the mission near Laprairie, Canada. Resisting attempts that she marry, she was the first of her people to make the vow of virginity. Kateri died at a young age. Her face had been disfigured by smallpox since the age of four; a few minutes after her death, all traces of the scars disappeared. After her death, she appeared in a vision to one of the missionaries, asking him to write her story and spread her picture.

Her death was followed by an extraordinary renewal of devotion, fervor, and penance throughout the mission where she died, and miracles attributed to the intercession of this Lily of the Mohawks began to spread. She was always acclaimed as a saint of the people, but it was not until 1884, when the bishops of the Third Council of Baltimore petitioned the Holy See, that the official process for her beatification was begun.

Craft a key chain in a style adapted from Native American beadwork.

Indian-Style Beaded Keychain
Directions

Thread a needle onto each end of cord. Slip one end of the cord through the key ring and center

Supplies needed

1 split circle key ring

2 yards nylon cord

2 large upholstery or darning needles

pony beads

scissors

cigarette lighter or match

graph paper & pencil (optional)

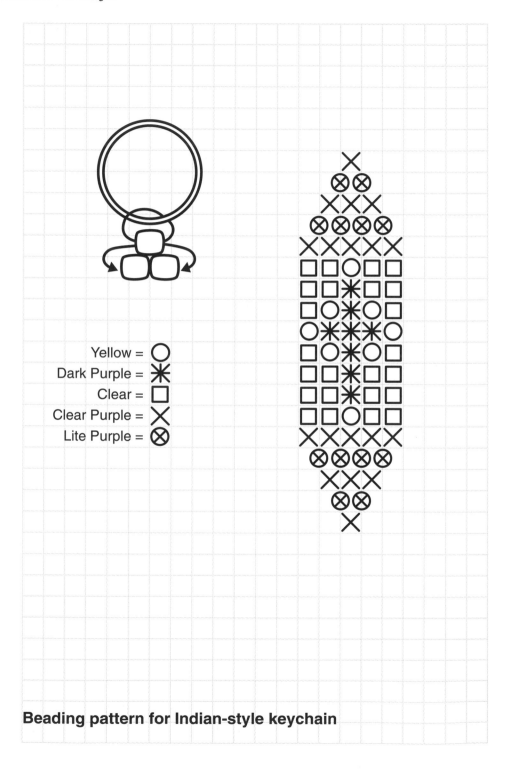

Yellow = ◯
Dark Purple = ✳
Clear = ▢
Clear Purple = ✕
Lite Purple = ⊗

Beading pattern for Indian-style keychain

on cord. String one bead on one side of cord. Just as you pull it off the needle, take the other needle and run it through the bead in the opposite direction, as shown the accompanying diagram. Each row will then be worked in the same way.

In the first row, you'll have 1 bead; in the second row, two; increase each row by 1 bead until there are 5 beads in each row. You'll string 10 rows of 5 beads each. Begin to decrease the rows by 1 bead until have strung a single bead (just as you started with). You'll have 18 rows in all.

Follow the pattern as shown in the diagram at left (a simple cross in yellow and purple surrounded by clear beads) or create your own. Push each row with your fingers to make certain it lies flat against the row before.

When you have added the last single bead, pull the cords taunt and tightly tie a square knot close to the bead. String an additional 5 beads on one side of the cord. Sew a tight knot through the end bead. Cut off excess cord; have an adult burn the end of the cord with a cigarette lighter and use the tip of the needle to press the hot nylon onto the

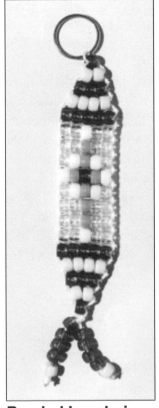

Beaded keychain

cord so the knot will not slip. Repeat the process on the second cord. If you have never worked with nylon cord, it is a good plan to try this burning technique on a piece of scrap cord a few times before working on your project. Do not touch the hot nylon; it burns like melted sugar!

July 26 — Feast of St. Ann

There is nothing really known for certain about Jesus' anonymous grandmother, but tradition assigns the name of Ann and a popular legend to the mother of Our Lady. Veneration to her began in the East about the fourth century, and during the Middle Ages it spread throughout the Christian world. Among her other patronages, St. Ann is known as the patroness of all women and, in particular, mothers.

The seafaring people of France have a special devotion to St. Ann, and one of the two greatest shrines to the saint is located at St. Anne d'Auray on the coast of the Bay of Biscay. Miraculous favors granted to sailors by St. Ann have been recorded in the archives there since the shrine's construction in 1623.

The Venerable Mother Theodore Guerin, foundress of the Sisters of Providence, was a native of Brittany and the daughter of a captain in the French navy. In 1842 on her return from a fundraising trip to France, the ship on which she sailed was in immediate danger of sinking in a terrible storm. Mother Theodore appealed fervently to St. Ann, and the ship was saved. In gratitude, Mother Theodore sent an ex voto offering to the shrine in France and obtained a statue of the saint for a small chapel at St. Mary of the Woods, Indiana. Special prayers of gratitude to the saint were recited by all the sisters. Later, one of the sisters who was also a native of Brittany directed the novices in decorating the interior of a small stone shrine chapel using designs of mussel and oyster shells set in soft plaster.

Sea shells have been popular for decoration from time immemorial.

St. Ann Victorian shell plaque

Throughout Christian history, the shell has been symbolic of Christ's baptism. A cockle shell sewn on one's hat was a sign that a pilgrim had successfully made it to the shrine of St. James of Compostello. From the Elizabethan age into the 19th century, shell grottoes and pavilions were fashionable on estates in France and England, and some shell work was used in chapels. The grottos were caves and, later, entire rooms decorated completely with shells. During the Victorian age, shell-encrusted mirrors and picture frames were immensely popular. In Germany, wreaths and flower arrangements were crafted from shells and placed in glass boxes in the cemetery.

Since not everyone lives close enough to the ocean to gather their own shells and since they are often expensive at the craft store, our Victorian-style wall plaque tribute to St. Ann is crafted of shell-shaped macaroni!

St. Ann Victorian Shell Plaque
Directions

Obtain the medallion or picture of St. Ann at a religious goods store. They are usually sold in a small plastic folder that contains the medallion and a prayer. If you can't find a medallion you can use a picture of the saint, but you will lose the monochrome effect.

Cut a 4" square of corrugated cardboard. Glue the medallion in the center with hot glue. If you are using a picture, cut an opening in your cardboard $1/8$" to $1/4$" smaller than your picture. Put a $3/4$" band of white craft-glue around the edge of the medallion and position large shells as close together as possible around the medallion with one tip just touching the edge of the cardboard. Add another band of glue outside the first and repeat the layer of shells. Continue in the same manner until you have reached the outside edge of the cardboard. Add more glue between the shells where there are gaps and fill in with small shells. Allow the edges of the shells to stick out from the edge slightly.

Allow project to dry overnight.

When project is thoroughly dry and there are no loose shells, spray with a flat finish paint. We chose a rosy pink. Allow to dry.

Supplies needed

- two sizes of shell-shaped macaroni; pieces $1/2$" and $3/4$" in length
- cardboard
- silver curtain ring
- 1 foot grosgrain ribbon, $1\frac{1}{2}$" wide, in chosen color
- white craft-glue
- hot-glue gun
- 16" thin cord or braid, in chosen color
- flat spray paint, in chosen color
- $1\frac{1}{2}$"x2" metal medallion of St. Ann, or substitute a small picture
- metallic silver paint
- stiff paintbrush

If you're using a picture instead of the medallion, you can glue it in place from the back at this point.

Beginning at the bottom of your plaque, hot-glue the cord, starting in the middle, around the entire outside of the plaque to hide the corrugated edge of the cardboard. Let dry.

Next, loop one end of the ribbon through the ring (about three inches) and glue together. Cut a "V" in the bottom of the ribbon. Position your plaque on the ribbon about an inch below the ring and hot-glue the plaque in place.

Using a stiff brush and silver paint, lightly brush over the top of the shells and the raised portion of the medallion to give a silvery accent. With your silvery glitter fabric paint, trace over the haloes of St. Ann and the child Mary. Carefully run a line of the paint around the edges of the shells closest to the medallion or picture. Make a tiny dot of silver glitter fabric paint at the tip end of some of the smaller shells for an additional accent.

August 19 — Blessed Isidore Bakanja

Blessed Isidore Bakanja, a native of what is now called Zaire, was attracted to faith in Christ as a teenager. The first Catholic of his region, out of love for Jesus and Mary, on his own he taught Christian prayer and truth to his companions. Because he would not reject the rosary and scapular which for him were signs of his Catholicism, he was mercilessly and savagely beaten by a Belgian colonist, until his back was a large, festering wound. After six months of excruciating pain, he forgave the man who had beaten him and promised to pray for him in heaven.

On August 19, 1909, this humble lay catechist, who had been bedridden and unable to walk for months and who for some days had been in a deep delirium, suddenly arose and walked into the banana patch near the house where he was staying. He had his rosary in his hand. So often before he had walked to pray in quiet; one last time this son of Our Lady was allowed to pray. He returned, lay down, participated in a prayer session and, after eating, he soon afterwards quietly died. Blessed Isidore was beatified in 1994 as a martyr for the scapular.

African Madonna and Child Leaf Picture

Make our African Madonna and Child Picture to remind you of Blessed Isidore's devotion to Our Lady. The picture is done in a style popular in Kenya. The picture is made from thin pieces of leaf and bark glued onto fabric.

Directions

Gather old leaves from your yard, or press leaves as described for the floral bookmark on page 122 of this book. You need various shades of

---

Supplies needed

- dried leaves
- scraps of textured brown paper (optional)
- gold embroidery thread and needle (optional)
- 5"x7" piece of unbleached muslin or other thin, off-white fabric
- white craft-glue
- tweezers
- sharp scissors
- 5"x7" simple wooden picture frame

brown and tan, and different textures, although all should be relatively thin. They can't be crumbly-dry, or you won't be able to cut them.

Copy our pattern on the next page (use as is, or enlarge on a copier to 110% or greater for a bigger picture) and cut out the pieces. Trace around each piece on a piece of leaf. If you haven't located enough variety in your leaves, you can use scraps of brown paper. If you have difficulty with leaves shattering, soak them in warm water for a few minutes and pat dry with a paper towel before continuing. Starting with the Virgin's face, glue the pieces to your fabric with white craft-glue; you can use your finger to spread the glue evenly across the back of each piece. A tweezers will help you place the pieces.

On our original, sent to us by a priest friend in Africa, the halos are made from the tiniest pieces of cut leaf. If this proves too tedious for you, you can embroider the haloes with gold embroidery thread in either a simple running stitch or in a chain stitch. Allow the picture to dry completely before framing.

African Madonna and Child leaf picture

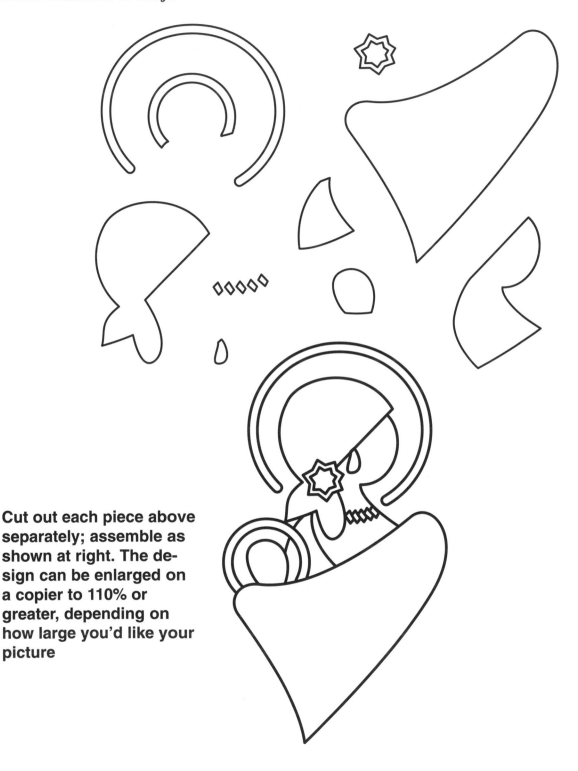

Cut out each piece above separately; assemble as shown at right. The design can be enlarged on a copier to 110% or greater, depending on how large you'd like your picture

September and October

Emproidered pictures of Our Lady

September 8 — Our Lady's Birthday

Nine months after the feast of the Immaculate Conception, the Church celebrates the feast of the Nativity of the Blessed Virgin. As a birthday remembrance for Our Lady, craft an embroidered picture of your favorite title for her. This type of art has been popular in Spain and other countries for years.

Embroidered Picture of Our Lady
Directions

Obtain a colored print (on thin paper) of your favorite picture of Our Lady. Using fine stitches, "paint" in part of the picture by filling in colored areas with like-colored thread. Your embroidery will usually be only on the clothing or the crown or halo; objects in the background are not usually stitched.

Use single threads of the finest shiny embroidery thread; there is no need to make knots at the back because the picture will later be glued to a backing. Metallic gold or silver thread makes a nice accent.

Most of the pictures I have seen done in this manner used primarily the satin, chain, and simple running stitch. It is best to attempt a small, postcard-sized picture for your first attempt at this

Supplies needed

thin needle

scissors

various thin, shiny embroidery threads

colored print of Our Lady

white craft-glue

stiff cardboard to back picture

craft. It is delicate and the finest needles must be used to avoid tearing the paper.

When you have embroidered as many accents as you wish, glue stiff cardboard to the back. Matte or frame your picture to hang.

October 3 — St. Thérèse of Lisieux

In 1897, a young nun died of tuberculosis in the Carmel of Lisieux after bravely sticking to her spiritual "little way" of simple trust in and love for God during the nine years of her residency there. After her death, her autobiography was printed and its success was sensational, with instant appeal in every language into which it was translated. Veneration for the obscure and unknown nun spread like wildfire and miracles and answers to prayer were attributed to her intercession. Canonized in 1925, little Thérèse Martin became the most popular saint of modern times. She had shown that sainthood is attainable by anyone. The revolutionary pattern for life that she set in her "little way" was simply to do small things and to discharge one's daily duties in a perfect spirit of love of God.

Good deed beads

According to several biographers, the child Thérèse was given a string of beads with which to count her acts of love accomplished for God.

In earlier years, similar strings were used by a number of religious orders and known as "virtue beads." The sisters often pinned the beads to their habits. During the day, each time they performed an act of love or sacrifice, they pulled a bead. The goal was to move all the beads by the end of the day. Even young children can make and enjoy this project, and the beads can double as a single decade rosary for busy people whose prayer time is often interrupted.

Good Deed Beads

Directions

See the diagram below for help on stringing the beads. First, string the medal, cross, or heart onto the cord and move it to the center. Tie an overhand knot in the cord and pull it tight to the top of the medal.

String the beads, 1 at a time, by running both ends of the cord through the hole from the opposite sides, as in the diagram. As you add each bead, move it down close to the previous bead to keep the two ends of the cord even.

When all 10 beads have been strung, hold the 2 ends of the cord together evenly and tie a knot, leaving a space of about 2 inches from the last bead so that you have room to move the beads up and down along the cord. The crossed cords inside the beads will hold each in place as you move one bead at a time for each good deed or prayer.

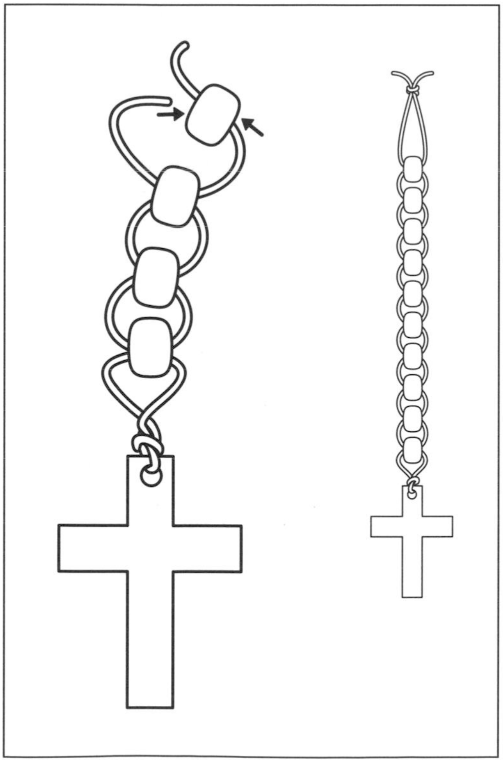

Trim the ends of the cord. If using a nylon-type cord, an adult should burn the ends of the cord slightly to prevent them slipping through the knot; a small dab of glue can prevent unraveling of other types of cord.

You may add a small safety pin at the top to attach the beads to a dress or coat if you wish.

Hint: If you are making these as a class or group project, buy the beads at a craft shop; if you only want to make 1 or 2, it may be cheaper to look in the hair accessories section of the local dollar or grocery store. Wooden beads could also be used if they have large holes.

Stringing pattern for beads

Supplies needed
1 yard of cord, string, or lacing
10 pony beads
1 inexpensive medal, cross, or heart

October 7 — Feast of the Holy Rosary

Beads have been present in all known cultures throughout history. They have been used as adornment, talismans, money, and to display wealth and power.

The word "bead" derives from the Anglo-Saxon "*biddan*," to pray, and "*bede*," meaning prayer. Prayer beads are used by more than half of the world's religions: Hinduism, Buddhism, Islam, as well as Catholicism.

In the West, where the medieval church frowned on forms of adornment, it was not until the 16th century that bead jewelry was worn by women as well as men to enhance beauty and as a sign of status. From the Renaissance, beads have been sewn onto clothing for decoration. Today, embroidery beads have become a staple of glamorous fashion garments.

Beads have been made in all types of material, natural and man-made. They have also found other ecclesiastical uses. *Majolica* beads, earthenware glazed to look opaque, were made in Italy in the 1920s. Special beads were made in old Russia to be sewn on

Several styles of pull rosaries

the altar fabrics. These were decorated with religious mottos. Beads crafted as tiny bells were made in Germany to be sewn on the traditional pre-Lent carnival costumes.

The practice of using a string of beads as an aid in meditation and prayer is an ancient one. Early monks, wishing to say a certain number of prayers, counted the prayers by moving small pebbles or stones from one container to another. Later, strings of beads were used for counting. During the Middle Ages, the rosary (which we know today as the Dominican rosary) evolved and became one of the most popular sacramentals of the church. The word "rosary" is from the Latin *rosarium*, or rose garden. It signified a wreath or garland and was seen as a special favor or presentation to Our Lord and Our Lady. The word "chaplet," from the Old French *chaplet*, and the Latin word *corona* also mean a wreath or crown.

Today, the words rosary, chaplet, corona, and beads are used interchangeably to refer to prayer devotions which use special strings of beads to aid Catholics in meditation. A myriad of chaplets honor Our Lord, Our Lady, the Trinity, the angels or saints, and new chaplets are composed to honor and spread devotion to a particular mystery or aspect of our religion.

Below, we give a new pattern for the Dominican rosary.

The Pull Rosary

This rosary is inexpensive to make, attractive, easy enough for a six-year-old to construct, and best of all, if you get interrupted while praying, you can return to find the place where you stopped.

Directions

See the diagram on page 88 for help in assembling the rosary. Fold the cord in half and push the loop through the hole at the top of the cross. Run the loose ends of the cord through the loop as in diagram A, pulling tight. Thread both ends of the cord through these beads: 1 black, 3 clear, 1 black, and the red bead to form the introductory portion of the rosary.

Separate the 2 cords and string the remainder of the beads, one at a time, by running each end of the cord through the hole, from opposite sides, as in diagram B on page 88. Use this pattern: 10 clear beads, 1 black bead. Repeat this 5 times; but after the 5th set of clear beads, do not use a black bead.

> **Supplies needed**
>
> 53 clear (or first color) pony beads
>
> 6 black (or second color) pony beads
>
> 1 red (or third color) heart-shaped bead
>
> 1 crucifix or cross with hole at top
>
> 2 yards thin nylon cord

As you add each bead, move it down tightly to the previous bead to keep the 2 ends of the cords even.

When all beads have been strung, hold the 2 ends of the cords together evenly and leave a space of about ½-inch from the last bead so that you have room to move the beads up and down along the cords. Run what's left of the cords back through the first beads and through the hole in the cross.

Secure with several half hitches or other suitable knot.

Burn the ends of the cord to keep them from unraveling. If a child or young person is making this project, have an adult assist with this part. Clip off excess cord and hide the knot by sliding the introductory beads to cover.

As you pray, the crossed cords will hold each bead in place as you move one bead at a time. If you are interrupted in your prayers, you can see immediately on your return where you left off.

Hint: Any type of bead with a large hole can be used. A bead of a different color or an elongated bead may be substituted for the heart bead. Although a different type of cord could be used, nylon is the strongest and will withstand constant use better.

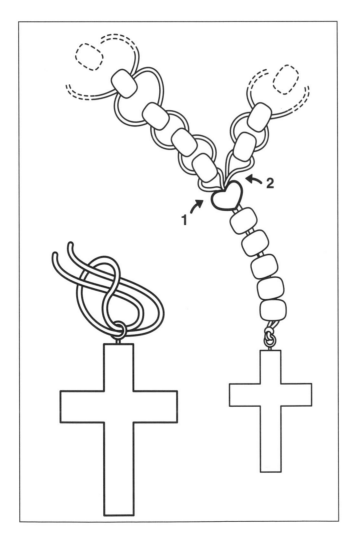

Stringing pattern for pull rosaries. At left, how to secure the cross. Right, how to string the beads: 1. Begin stringing. 2. After all the beads are strung, leave ½-inch of cord between the last bead and the heart bead. Run the remainder of the cord back through the heart and round beads, and secure to the hole in the cross with a secure knot or two.

November

November 1 — All Saints' Day
New Mexican-Style Retablos

The Church at Antioch kept a commemoration of all holy martyrs on the first Sunday after Pentecost. The feast spread through the Eastern Church; by the seventh century it was kept everywhere as a public holiday. The feast of "All Holy Martyrs" was introduced in the West by Pope Boniface IV; in 844 Pope Gregory IV transferred it to November 1. The other saints began to be included in the memorial, and Pope Sixtus IV established it as a holy day for the entire Latin Church.

Catholicism arrived in New Mexico in the late 16th century along with the Spanish Conquistadores. Missionaries began evangelization of the native peoples. New Mexico was a rough and rugged terrain, and the population was isolated and widely scattered. This isolation dictated a unique art form that grew and changed through time with limited outside contact.

The iconography of the *retablos*, paintings on wood or tin, served as a catechism for the people. Paintings from Spain were few and far between, so the native artists, called *santeros*, copied them, imparting their own style to the subjects. *Bultos*, three-dimensional saints carved from wood, took the place of the European statues, which were almost impossible to obtain. Carved by untrained artists, these *santos* have a style and flavor of their own.

The *santeros* of old New Mexico made a living creating saints for personal and group worship. They were artisans and teachers, and on their travels they shared their stories from community to community.

Today, a number of *santeros* continue making the *retablos* and *bultos*, and any visitor to Santa Fe can find a myriad of them in the galleries of the city. To dismiss them as "folk art" is a gross oversimplification.

Charlie Carrillo is a modern-day *santero*. A prolific and award-winning artist, Charlie has never formally studied art. He fits the traditional *santero* mold, however, in accompanying his art with stories about the *santos* and the traditions from the Spanish colonial period in New Mexico. Carrillo says, "*Santos* are objects of art, but they are also objects of devotion. They are in the stories of all of us." Being a *santero* in the strictest interpretation is not just teaching, sharing, and making art; it is also a way of life. The *santos* were made to be a part of everyday life.

New Mexican-style retablos

Because of a lack of priests to minister to the people, the Roman Catholic Penitente Brotherhood began in northern New Mexico and spread to southern Colorado. Known today simply as Penitentes, this association of laymen is dedicated to an active life of service while living a life of devotion to the suffering and death of Jesus Christ. Originally organized for pious observances involving the expiation of sin through prayer and bodily penance, and for mutual aid, the brotherhood became a conservative cultural force, preserving language, lore, customs, and faith.

Carrillo is a member of the Penitente *morada*, or meeting place of the brotherhood, in Abiquiú. Here he first became enthralled with the beauty of the *santos*. His passion for the picturesque icons drove him to do intense research, learning more about the various saints, their history and stories, and about the traditional way of crafting them. He carved the first of his nearly four thousand works of religious art in 1977.

In Hispanic eschatology, there is a strong communion between the departed and the living. Anglo-Americans who are unused to the Spanish penitential nature and unfamiliar with this communion are sometimes uneasy about the *santos*. Carrillo says, "This is because of the way we live with our *santos*, or the way the *santos* live with us. Our tradition is that *santos* are a part of our lives, not just something we hang on our wall, not just something we look to maybe every third day. But rather we talk to our *santos*. They are part of our lives. We don't just live with our saints. They live with us. We invite them into our homes to live with us." When asked what makes a *santo* so sacred in New Mexico, Carrillo will tell you, "It's the people's love for their devotions. A *santo* is only a piece of artwork among our people until he is blessed. Then the reverence, the devotion given, separates him as a piece of sacred work — as simple, as bad, or as ugly, or as beautiful as he is — from a piece in a gallery that's not blessed."

You can make one or a number of these New Mexican-style *retablos* to celebrate All Saints'. We provide patterns (on pages 163-67) for St. Ignatius, St. Martin de Porres, St. Patrick, and two views of Our Lady: Our Lady of the Sleeve (Sorrows), and a typical New Mexican pose where Our Lady is sitting in a chair holding a dove representing the Holy Ghost. Or create your own.

A particularly good project would be to craft the patron saint of each person in the family and display them at All Saints' and on the saint's feast day, or display them all year. Before you groan and say you can't possibly draw, remember my aunt's advice: "*Can't* never did nothin'!" All *retablos* were made by folk artists who were never formally trained in art.

You can make an original drawing or alter one of our patterns. Begin by looking up your saint and reading his or her story. In art, saints are always represented with certain symbols and there are books available on this subject; you may find such a book in your local or church library.

The story of the saint will give you ideas. For example, St. Patrick was a bishop, so he is shown in art wearing a bishop's mitre (hat) and there is generally a shamrock included in pictures of him, representative of how he used this humble plant to explain the concept of the Trinity to the unlettered pagans of early Ireland. St. Joseph can be shown with a lily for his purity or with a hammer and saw, representative of his occupation as a carpenter. St. Barbara is pictured with the tower where her father imprisoned her; St. Christopher is usually shown carrying the Christ Child across the water and with a staff in his hand which, according to his legend, he later planted.

The research on this project is educational and fun for a family or class.

Supplies needed

rectangular piece of wood

Hint: You can use the end of a grape crate; see "Home Altar" on page 62. If you use scrap lumber, the pieces should be no more than 1" thick.

saw (optional)

picture hanger

Hint: Use the pull top from a soda can for a no-cost hanger.

hammer and small nail

gesso

sandpaper

carbon paper

acrylic or tempera paints, including flesh color

fine-line permanent black marker

clear acrylic spray, matte finish

patterns in the Appendix

Directions

Begin by cutting the corners off your plaques if you wish. Nail a hanger to the back. Paint the front and sides of your plaque with gesso. (Remember to cover your work area well and wash brushes immediately in cool water, as gesso hardens like plaster.) Let dry, sand, and apply a second coat of gesso.

Enlarge one of our patterns (found in the Appendix, pages 163-67) to fit the size of your board, either using a copy machine with enlarging capability or using the instructions on page 179-80. Put a piece of carbon paper between the pattern and board and trace over the design. Paint all the large areas with acrylic or tempera paint. Shading is not necessary, but a tiny bit of red paint thinned with water can make cheeks rosy, and a tiny bit of color mixed with white can be added for an attractive shading on clothing. Allow paint to dry thoroughly. Then, using a fine-line permanent black marker, go over the lines of the pattern to outline your *santo*.

After your *retablo* is thoroughly dry, coat with a clear acrylic spray. Reread the hints for spray painting found in the introduction to this book before spraying. If your final coat is not done properly, you can ruin your entire project!

November 2 — All Souls' Day, or *Día de Muertos*

Unlike Halloween, which is based on pagan beliefs and traditions, *Día de Muertos* is not simply "sanitized witchcraft." The Mexican celebration of All Souls' is one of the most sacred and revered days in the Mexican cycle of feasts. It stems from the ancient pre-Colombian belief that as long as a person was remembered by family and friends, that person continued to live. In celebrating the dead, they were kept alive.

All Souls' Day, a memorial feast commemorating in a common celebration all the souls of the faithful departed, was first begun at the Abbey of Cluny in 998. In 1003, it was recommended and approved by Pope Sylvester II, and from the 11th to the 14th century the feast gradually spread throughout Europe. In the Western church, the feast was set for November 2, so that the memories of all the souls, both of the saints in heaven and the souls of those in purgatory, could be celebrated on two successive days. This could more clearly express the Christian belief in the communion of saints. (The Eastern rites commemorate the faithful departed during the Easter season.) For Christ and those united in His Body the dead are alive; human solidarity reaches beyond death. The Church is the communion of the "holy ones" or "saints" who dwell on earth, in heaven, and in purgatory (CCC 946-962). Each act of love profits all those who are united in Christ, just as every sin harms them (CCC 953).

Throughout the world, numerous customs and pious traditions were associated with the celebrations in honor of the dead. Almost all ethnic traditions include special prayers, decorations, foods, lights, and the visiting and cleaning of graves. Some groups distribute food to the poor on this day, and others visit graves of the "forgotten" ones, graves that would otherwise remain neglected and unadorned. In a number of places worldwide, there is the pious belief that the souls of the dead return to earth at this time. None of the traditions can match those of Mexico in their abundance of joyful and colorful customs.

In Mexico, on the Day of the Dead, the people laugh, play, and joke with death; for them, it is an affirmation of the ultimate life. *Día de Muertos* is an enrichment of the doctrine of the communion of saints, and its celebration can deepen this aspect of our faith.

The celebration begins on November 1 when the souls of the *angelitos* — children — are remembered. On November 2, deceased adults are honored. Folklore tells that the spirits return to earth to visit, so elaborate preparations are made to welcome them with deep reverence and a great deal of warmth and humor. In some parts of Mexico, offerings of bread and water are hung outside the houses or placed in a corner of the church on October 27 for the spirits that have no one to greet them and no home to visit.

At this time of year, families go to the cemeteries to clean and weed. They decorate with flowers, both real and paper. In some parts of southern Mexico, the streets near the cemetery are literally paved with flowers. Flower wreaths, known as *coronas* or *crucitas*, are placed on every grave. Candles are numerous; these light the way for the souls to come and visit with their family. The people sometimes hold all-night vigils at the cemetery. The men drink and talk while the women sit by the grave and pray. The people spend the following day at the cemetery in the company of the dead, but also enjoying the company of the living. Mariachis play favorite music and the people talk, eat, and drink.

We need reminders of our supernatural solidarity with the deceased. Praying for the dead begins with remembering the dead. The *ofrenda*, or home altar, is a visual way to bring the dead to mind in order to pray for them.

The *ofrenda* commemorates the dead of individual families. These are special altars constructed in homes and sometimes in the *camposanto* (cemetery). The commemorative altars are covered with black cloth and decorated with *papel picado*, or cut-paper. The altars include flowers, candles, food, and anything that is a special reminder, or was especially loved by, the family dead. Usually, photos of the dead are set on the altar. Special toys and images of skeletons abound. Traditional foods include *mole* (a spicy chicken dish), rich candies such as *leche quemada* (milk candy), sugared pumpkin, and *pan de muertos* (bread of the dead). Popular shapes for the bread are the forms of men and women, a skull and crossbones, or a volcano spewing tears. On *ofrendas* dedicated to children who have died, there are special toys such as a tiny coffin whose skeleton occupant pops up when a string is pulled. Masks, puppets, and small clay figurines of skeletons in various dress and poses are also added to the *ofrenda*.

Calaveras, or skulls, come in many sizes. Skulls made of sugar are decorated fancifully with glitter and icing. Sometimes names are piped on with icing and the children exchange them as gifts.

The word "*calaveras*" has the double meaning of "skulls" and "scatterbrain." It is also the word for satirical poems. Another traditional activity is the giving of these poems from one friend to another, much as we exchange cards on St. Valentine's feast day. The *calaveras* often poke fun at politicians or other professionals and are elaborately illustrated with pictures of skeletons laughing and having a good time.

José Guadalupe Posada (1852-1913) was a Mexican artist with a great talent for illustrating the life and character of his countrymen. Although he died relatively unrecognized, he was the inspiration for a number of Mexico's most famous modern artists. He and his publisher were fearless crusaders who fought for reforms, and whose scathing caricatures of dishonest politicians constantly kept them in hot water. Posada is particularly known for his illustrations of the calaveras filled with grinning, dancing cadavers miming every conceivable activity in human existence. Today, copies of his work are often seen at the *Día de Muertos* public celebrations held in some cities of the United States. His wild skeleton partygoers adorn paper goods and tee-shirts. Undoubtedly, Posada would be pleased at how his art is helping to publicize one of Mexico's most important feasts.

The custom of the *ofrenda* is one worth adopting in any Catholic home. It can provide a powerful visual stimulus of prayers for and remembrance of the dead. In addition, the joyful humor and familiarity with death as expressed through the sugar skulls and skeleton toys can help remind us that although our loved ones are no longer present physically, death has not stolen them from us because they are alive in God and in us. Thus, in addition to serving as a prayer reminder, the *ofrenda* can also help achieve a form of closure for those who are grieving from a recent loss.

This year, why not consider adding the tradition of the ofrenda to your family celebrations? A number of parishes have adapted this custom to celebrate the lives of the deceased members of the parish. You may wish to check with your pastor to see if your parish could adopt the custom.

Your home altar may be as simple or elaborate as you choose. Place a black or purple cloth on a small table and display photos or other mementoes of the deceased members of your own family. *Papel picado* may be made by simply folding and cutting tissue, much as you would make a paper snowflake, or use our pattern. Candles should be added to symbolize the light of Christ. Add a crucifix or statue, flowers, and a plate of candy. Attend Mass as a family on All Souls' Day. Invite friends and relatives to share the food from the altar and to pray for the family dead. Celebrate! Because He lives, we too shall live.

Papel Picado

Papel Picado is the Hispanic version of cut-paper work, a craft known all over the world. Fanciful and elaborate designs cut from paper (*wycinanki*) are used in Poland much as we would use wallpaper; they are pasted to the wall. In Germany, the name for cut-paper is *scherenschnitte*; decorative paper cut-outs are made and backed with a contrasting paper, then framed as decorations. The Oriental countries use decorative cut-paper in a number of ways and some of the most elaborate cuttings are quite expensive. We cut a skeleton design to decorate our *ofrenda*.

Supplies needed

purple or other colored tissue-paper

pattern in the Appendix

small, very sharp scissors with points

paper clips

Directions

Fold a sheet of tissue paper in half sideways to make a long strip. Fold in half the other direction to form a smaller rectangle and in half once again. Secure folds by placing paper clips along the edges in several places. Sheets of colored tissue don't come in a standard size, so you will need to enlarge your pattern (on a copier with enlarging capability or by using the instructions on page 12) to the size to fit your paper. Our full sheet, when folded in half 3 times, made a rectangle about 7"x10".

Cut out the open portions of the pattern, found on page 168, along the dotted lines with sharp scissors.

Then place the pattern over the folded tissue and carefully trace the open parts with a pencil. Using sharp scissors, cut out the open portions as you did with the pattern. It is easiest if you fold the paper slightly and make your beginning cut in the center of the portion you are cutting out. Then cut to your pencil mark and continue around that part.

When finished, remove paper clips and unfold carefully.

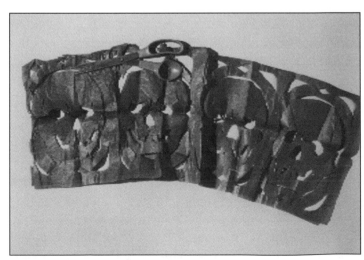

Cut-paper skeleton heads

Wooden Skeleton

Robbie, age six, wanted a big skeleton for the door, so his mother Lorraine made a pattern and used her scroll saw to cut it out of wood. He's perfect on the door at Halloween or for the wall to celebrate *Día de Muertos*. Lorraine sent Joanna the pattern, and Joanna made one for me with a little help from four-year-old Austin. After November, mine hangs at the side of a bookshelf where he can only be seen from one spot in the kitchen. He's always good for a startled jump and a good laugh when an unsuspecting guest happens to stand at that certain spot!

Directions

Enlarge patterns, found on pages 169-72, to the size you want, and trace onto the soft pine lumber. Any size of 1"-thick board will do; you can use scraps from other projects for this.

Cut out pieces. Paint with gesso. Gesso gives a nice, flat finish, but you can give it a coat of white paint for a different finish. Use a black permanent marker to draw features and outline the bones as shown on the pattern on page 173.

Screw a large eye hook at the top of skull for hanging, and another large hook at the bottom center of skull for the neck. Screw a small eye hook at the end of each bone (except hands and feet). With pliers, open one of the small hooks gently and hook it through the matching hook as shown in diagram. Continue until your skeleton is completely linked. Hung on the door, your skeleton will give a satisfying clunking sound each time the door is opened.

Supplies needed

- 1"-thick soft pine lumber, any size; scraps will suffice
- scroll saw; hand or electric
- 2- ½" eye-hooks
- 29- ⅜" eye-hooks
- gesso
- white paint (optional)
- paintbrush
- permanent black marker
- pliers
- patterns in the Appendix

Paper Skeleton Puppet

If you like, you can also use our pattern to make a paper skeleton puppet. Draw the pattern on heavy white card-stock paper. Punch holes and use paper brads to connect the sections. Punch a hole in top of head, hands, and feet, and tie strings through them. Tie the other end of the strings to a dowel rod. You can move his hands and legs by lifting the string.

November 3 — St. Martin de Porres

St. Martin de Porres was born in Lima, Peru, in 1579, the natural child of a Spanish knight and a free black woman from Panama. Although he acknowledged his children, Martin's father left them largely in the care of their mother. Even as a child Martin had a reputation for charity. At the age of 12, he was apprenticed to a barber-surgeon, where he learned the healing arts. At 15, he became a Dominican lay brother at the Rosary Convent in Lima. He was in charge of distributing to the poor the monastery's alms, which he is said to have miraculously multiplied. He assisted in founding a number of charitable institutions, and cared for the slaves brought to Peru from Africa. He had a love for nature and a tender regard for all animals, including vermin. One of the charming legends about the saint is that he was once overheard telling the mice that they must leave the monastery as they were causing too much damage, but that they could take up residence in the barn and he would see that they were fed.

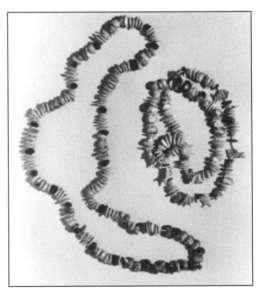

Puerto Rican seed necklaces

The miraculous was commonplace in the life of this saint, and he was favored with a number of mystical gifts, including bilocation. Martin is the patron of social justice.

Puerto Rico is the smallest, eastern-most island of the Greater Antilles, in the Caribbean Sea. A green and fertile island, it was originally inhabited by the Tainos, a peaceful, agricultural people who left today's islanders with a heritage of love for the land. Catholicism traveled to the island with the Spaniards at the time of the Conquest. Later, slaves were brought from Africa. The culture of Puerto Rico is a mixture of African, Indian, and Spanish influences.

My friend William Velez remembers the happy fiestas held in honor of the saints in his home town of Yauco, Puerto Rico, when he was a child. St. Martin de Porres was very popular. One of William's aunts made clothing to simulate that of the saint and wore it in his honor. At the fiesta, a large procession would be held, and the statue of the saint carried about the town. Necklaces made of native seeds and beans would be presented to the saint as offerings, and his hands would be full of strings of the brightly-colored, natural "beads." Also, the decorated platform on which the statue was carried would be covered with these traditional seed necklaces.

Necklaces made from native seeds and beans are still sold in the tourist shops. One of the most popular seeds is from the *camándula* plant and is called "Job's tears." The word *"camándula"* means rosary beads, and these seeds have also been used for rosaries for many years.

We can learn from Puerto Rico to use what is in our environment. Look both indoors and out for seeds you can use to make a necklace. If you discover pretty seeds outside, ask your local garden shop to identify them if you are worried about the possibility of their being poisonous. Decorate around a small statue or picture of St. Martin de Porres or your favorite saint with a string of seeds or beans. Or make a necklace in colors to match your favorite outfit.

Puerto Rican Seed Necklaces

Directions

Prepare lemon (or orange or grapefruit) rind: Remove fruit pulp from a lemon and soak the rind in water for several hours. (I discovered how to do this one morning when I dumped out a glass of iced tea that had set overnight. I noticed the lemon was very soft and pliable.) With a sharp knife, carefully scrape away most of the white pulp next to the yellow rind, leaving only a paper-thin layer. With sharp scissors cut the rind into tiny fish shapes or crosses. For the fish, punch a tiny hole for an eye with the tip of an ice pick or meat skewer.

If you aren't planning on working with them

Supplies needed

- sharp, thin needle
- heavy thread — we used a cotton crochet thread, but fishline or heavy sewing thread will suffice
- thimble (optional, but helpful)
- dishrag
- small corrugated-cardboard box
- microwave and cup, or pan and stove
- seeds
- for rind additions: lemon, orange, or grapefruit rind
- sharp scissors and knife
- pair of fish-hook earring-wires from craft store
- clear acrylic spray
- hot-glue gun and tweezers

that day, sew across the body of each fish, from top to bottom, with heavy thread. After stringing several this way, hang to dry; every few hours press each fish between thumb and forefinger to keep them from curling too much. If you work with them immediately after cutting, while they're still damp, stringing them in between the seeds on your necklace, you will still have to press each one to be sure they dry flat.

Gather the seeds you want to use. Coffee beans, dried Indian corn, sunflower seeds, allspice, cantaloupe, acorn squash, pumpkin, and watermelon are all good choices. You can also use almost any type of bean from your pantry.

We worked on a formica counter, using a brown paper grocery bag to pour our damp beads on.

Place each type of seed or bean in a coffee cup and cover with water. Microwave on high for 3 minutes. Remove from microwave, cover, and allow to stand until cool while you prepare the other seeds you will use. (The old-fashioned way, of course, is to boil the seeds. This still works fine if you have no microwave.)

Tie a knot in the end of your cord and string the seeds and beans in a pleasant pattern. Even after boiling, some seeds will be hard; when you put the needle into the seed, you can direct it toward the cardboard box and push the top of your needle with a thimble. That way, you can avoid jabbing the needle into your finger. A dishrag will help pull the needle through a particularly stiff seed or bean.

If you are stringing beans of the type you usually eat, be careful. Some of the prettiest ones will lose their colored skin if you boil or microwave them too long.

When your strings are long enough to slip over your head easily, hang them to air-dry for a few days. Make them a few inches longer than you want your finished string to be, because they will shrink as they dry. For this reason, do not tie your necklace until it is thoroughly dry.

November 11 — St. Martin of Tours

St. Martin was born at Sabaria, in what is now Hungary, about 316. The son of a pagan soldier, Martin entered the Roman army at the age of 15 and served for 20 years. A good officer, Martin lived frugally and often gave the remainder of his pay to charity. While still in the Roman army, he became a Christian catechumen. In 337, while stationed at Amiens, Martin was passing through the city one winter morning when he spied a beggar leaning against the city wall. Seeing that no one else was stopping to help, and having no money with him, Martin rode over on his fine horse and, cutting his cloak in half, he gave half of it to the beggar. That night in a happy dream, Martin had a vision of heaven; in the center of the Celestial Hosts stood the Savior, wrapped in a soldier's torn cloak.

Soon after this, Martin openly declared himself a Christian and requested baptism. He left the army and became a monk. He became a great evangelizer and preached against the Arian heresy. Over his protests, Martin was elected Bishop of Tours in 371. He was an extremely active missionary and he gained a reputation as a wonder-worker. He is known as the father of monasticism in France, and his fame spread far and wide, from Ireland to Africa and the East. He was one of the first holy men who was not a martyr to be publicly venerated as a saint. Martin died in 397.

In Spanish-speaking countries, St. Martin is known as *San Martín del Caballo* (St. Martin of the Horse) or *Caballero* (Knight.) His feast is still popularly celebrated today in many parts of Europe. He is the patron both of soldiers and peacemakers.

Friend Karin Murthough remembers the way St. Martin's feast was celebrated in her

St. Martin's lamp

home town of Mühlheim, Germany, when she was a child in the 1950s. Preparations began several days before, as the children made lanterns of sugar beets or paper to carry in the procession on November 11. The paper lanterns could be homemade or bought, and the children cut out pictures of St. Martin or his horse to paste on them.

In the early evening of his feast, a man dressed as the saint but wearing only half a cloak rode in the streets near the parish church. He carried a burlap sack filled with soft pretzels or rolls and led a procession. The children followed, holding up their lanterns on sticks and singing a song about feeding the hungry beggar. The children followed the saint as he rode through the old part of town and back to the church. Then they circled around the saint and he passed out the contents of his sack. The laughing, happy children fought to get close enough to the saint to make certain of receiving a pretzel or roll.

Make our St. Martin's lamp to light on his feast day, or to remind you of his charity throughout the year.

St. Martin's Lamp

Supplies needed

tall, clear-glass vigil candle

light-blue and yellow tissue paper

old magazine with glossy pages

clear wallpaper paste

spray glue*

clear or iridescent glitter

pattern on page 103

Directions

Cut out the shapes of five horses using old magazine pages. You don't have to find pictures of horses; try to find a page printed with fairly dark inks, and cut the outline of a horse, using the pattern on page 103. The pattern can be reduced or enlarged, depending on the size of your candle.

Then cut one-half of a sheet of each color tissue into small triangles that are about 2" tall with 1" bases. These do not have to be exact, nor do they have to be all exactly the same size. Work over waxed paper or on a counter that can be easily cleaned with water. This project is messy.

Glue the horse-shaped cut-outs to the candle in a random pattern using wallpaper paste. Do not place them lower than 2" from the bottom of the candle.

Wet a triangle with paste and begin completely covering the candle with the tissue-paper triangles, starting at the top. At the top of the candle, let the tissue-paper paper extend about ½" so you can fold them over and cover the rim of the candle.

Alternate your colors so that you have a pleasing pattern. The triangles should overlap slightly. Continue until the whole thing, including the horses, is covered; you should lap about ⅛" to ¼" under to the bottom to give a finished effect. Allow the candle to dry; clean the work area while you wait.

Spread a sheet of fresh waxed paper over your work area. Place your hand inside the candle to hold it while you spray the entire outside with spray glue.

If you do not have spray glue available, you can brush on white craft-glue that has been thinned with a little water. Pour clear, iridescent glitter over the glue, shaking excess onto the waxed paper for later return to the bottle. Allow candle to dry thoroughly before lighting.

Surprise! When you light St. Martin's "lamp" you can see his horse.

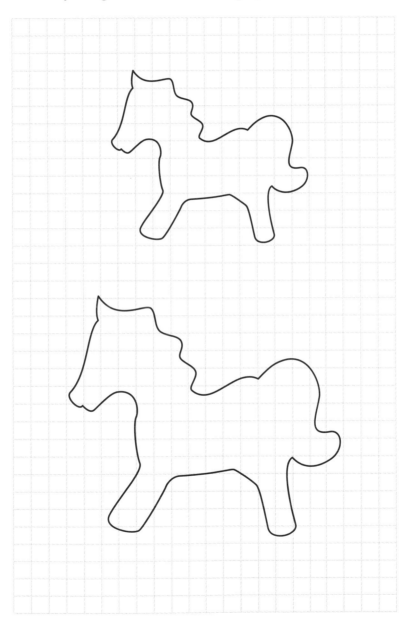

**Pattern
for
St.
Martin's
horse**

December

December 12— Feast of Our Lady of Guadalupe

In 1531, the Blessed Virgin Mary appeared to a humble Indian convert, Juan Diego, in Mexico, under the title of "Our Lady of Guadalupe." She asked that a church be built in her honor on the hill of Tepayac at the site of the apparition and instructed Juan to give this message to the bishop. Although Juan hurried to the bishop with the heavenly message, the bishop required a sign.

When Juan told the beautiful lady of the bishop's demand, she told him to pick the Castilian roses growing on the hill. This was miraculous for two reasons: 1) it was the wrong time of year for flowers to be blooming there, and 2) there were no native rosebushes in Mexico at this time. Nonetheless, the faithful Indian looked for, and found, the flowers the lady spoke of. Juan carefully carried the roses in his *tilma*, a scapular-type of garment made of *maguey* fiber.

Guadalupe scented frame

In the bishop's presence again, Juan opened the *tilma* and the roses cascaded to the floor. The bishop immediately knelt in front of Juan. The roses were only one sign; the beautiful portrait of herself that Our Lady left imprinted on Juan Diego's *tilma* was a much stronger sign. Juan's *tilma* remains today at the shrine of Our Lady of Guadalupe in Mexico City. Time and again the miraculous *tilma* has been studied, but no one has been able to explain how the portrait was impressed on the fabric.

Our Lady under the title "Virgin of Guadalupe" is the patroness of all the Americas. In the United States, her feast is celebrated on December 12.

Make a beautiful scented frame for a picture of Guadalupe to remind you of the Mother of the Americas.

Guadalupe Scented Frame

Directions

Using the rolling pin, roll out a ball of blue clay between two pieces of waxed paper until it is approximately ⅛" thick. Lay the laminated card on the clay and cut around the outside with a knife to make the back of your scented frame.

Place the clay on a piece of foil and bake at 300° for at least 45 minutes. Remove from heat and let cool.

Roll out a long "snake" of even thickness, about ¼" round, from blue clay. Working on waxed paper, lay the holy card down and put the "snake" around the rim of the card. With your fingers, press the clay against the laminated card to form a flat frame approximately ⅛" thick. Do not attempt to make the edges of the frame straight; they can have a slightly scalloped shape.

Carefully remove the frame from the card and put in on a piece of foil. Check to make certain the frame has not pulled out of shape by placing the card on top of it; realign it if necessary. Remove card.

Roll out a very thin snake of green clay and lay it along the right side and the bottom of the frame to form a vine. Make leaves by forming tiny teardrop shapes from green clay. Use a toothpick to help you place the leaves on the frame, as in the picture. Use the toothpick to draw a line down the middle of each leaf for a more realistic look.

Form tiny roses by making small balls of pink or red clay and pressing them flat between your fingers. You will need five petals for each open rose;

Supplies needed

Sculpey III modeling material

rolling pin

foil

waxed paper

toothpick

oven

a laminated holy card of Our Lady of Guadalupe

clear spray

hot-glue gun

rose fragrance oil

bottle of glittery gold or iridescent fabric paint (optional)

pleater-style drapery hanger

use the toothpick to help you place and press them against the clay. To form rosebuds, form a slightly larger ball of clay and flatten between fingers. Then, roll the circle up letting one side overlap the other. Put a tiny green leaf at the stem end of each bud. Form small bead-like balls of off-white clay and place 5 to 7 of them between the roses along the vine.

Bake the flowered frame in the oven at 300° for about 30 minutes.

When frame has cooled, spray with a light coat of clear acrylic spray to bring out the colors.

Place a small dab of hot glue in the center of the backing and press the laminated card against the glue to hold the picture in place. Carefully glue the flower frame over the picture. If you like, you can use glittery gold or iridescent fabric-paint to highlight the flowers, leaves, or part of the picture.

Make a stand for your picture by bending the middle, hook part of a pleater drapery hanger backwards to form an easel-like leg. With a pair of pliers, turn about ¼" of the outside two prongs up to hold the picture more securely.

Place a few drops of rose fragrance oil on the back of your picture. The porous clay will absorb the oil readily. Store the picture tightly sealed in a plastic zipper-bag for a few days until the rose smell permeates the entire picture. Then display the picture for a visual and olfactory treat and a good reminder to ask Our Lady to protect our homes, our families, and our country.

December 28 — Feast of the Holy Innocents

Billie Walter is the creator of the dolls of Shepherd's Flock. After years of working with preschool children, Billie created dolls of Jesus, Mary, Joseph, angels, and saints. She thought, "Instead of playing with fictional heroes like Batman, why not let children play with holy heroes?"

In addition to her teaching experience, Billie has worked with battered children. She noticed that these children often find comfort in tightly clutching a stuffed animal or doll. Sadly, for poor children, soft toys are often not available.

After seeing a television special about the children in orphanages in Romania, Billie created a pocket-sized baby Jesus doll which, unlike her line of larger dolls, is not for sale. Instead, she has made hundreds of them which she has given away. The dolls are blessed and given to children in need of comfort, along with a card that tells the story of "A Very Special Baby." A Claretian priest friend and Billie's son carried a number of the dolls to Russia with them, to give to children there. A Protestant pastor she knows gives them to battered children at the facility where he is a chaplain. Other people have asked for the baby Jesus dolls. Soft and comforting, easily held in a child's hand, the little doll seems to talk, softly and gently, to the children.

Why not honor the Holy Innocents, those children killed by Herod in his attempt to murder Our Lord as an infant, by making some of these baby Jesus dolls? Have them blessed and give them, along with the story card, to some innocent children who need the comfort of a baby Jesus to hold.

The baby Jesus dolls are good for pediatric wards of hospitals, for homeless ministries, for the offices of Christian psychologists and doctors, and for the elderly in convalescent homes. They can be made from scraps or from unbleached muslin for under 10 cents each.

Baby Jesus Doll

Directions

Cut out two oval shapes per doll, using the provided pattern on the next page, from any fabric that is light in color and washable. Place the face template about 1/3 of the way down from the top of the oval and paint on the face. Use flesh-colored paint, tinting darker for other nationalities by adding a bit of brown paint. Paint should be thinned a little with water so that it will be softer.

Next, stencil the body, first thinning the paint as for the face. Placing the arc shape over the baby's head, squeeze dots of gold glitter paint directly from the bottle. With a firm brush, spread it around to make a glow around the little head.

When the paint is completely dry, outline body as shown on the diagram. Use fine-line blue and black permanent markers.

Paint on the hair, freehand, as in the sample, using thinned brown paint.

With the fine-point black marker, add the eyes, nose, and mouth. The face looks sweeter if it is placed on the bottom half of the head, low, as if the baby had his head down. The smaller the features, it seems, the sweeter the look. You might want to

Supplies needed

tag board or file folder to make pattern

stiff plastic to make painting template

light-colored, washable fabric

acrylic paints

gold-glitter fabric paint

fine-point blue and black permanent markers

needle and thread

poly-fil stuffing

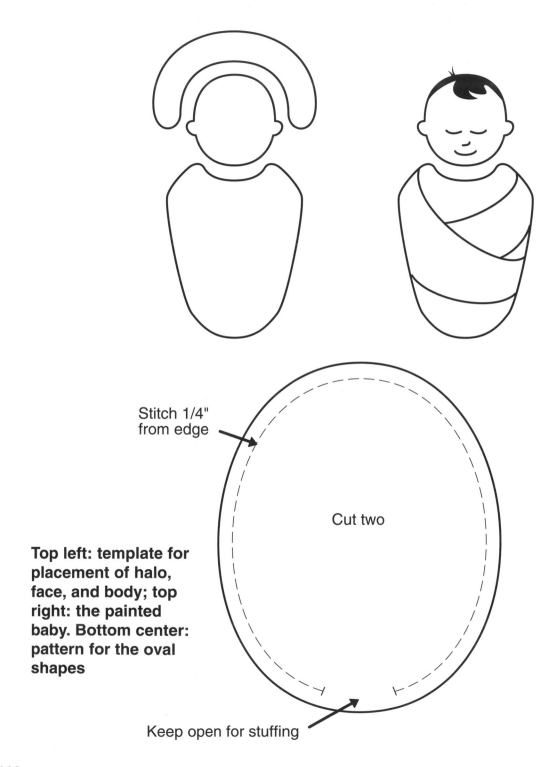

Stitch 1/4"
from edge

Cut two

Top left: template for placement of halo, face, and body; top right: the painted baby. Bottom center: pattern for the oval shapes

Keep open for stuffing

practice on paper before beginning your project.

Using carefree little strokes, paint hay with thinned straw-colored paint. On the back, paint a small cross with brown paint, and more little hay-like strokes with the straw color.

Place the right sides face-to-face and sew the ovals together, either by machine or by hand, leaving an opening on one side for stuffing. Polyfil is the best stuffing, but you can use anything that is soft. Stuff and stitch the side opening closed.

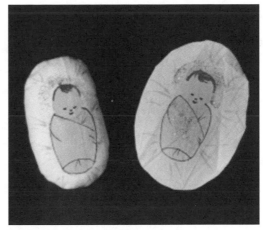

Baby Jesus dolls

Type Billie's story "A Very Special Baby" on a sheet of paper and photocopy to give away with the baby Jesus dolls.

A Very Special Baby

Many years ago, a very special baby was born in Bethlehem. His mother, Mary, held him and loved him and wrapped him in a blanket. Then she laid him down in a manger. They were staying in a stable because they could find no rooms in the village inn.

Mary's husband Joseph stood nearby. He was very happy to see the new baby.

Mary and Joseph named the baby Jesus. They knew he was the son of God and they taught him everything they know about God. Jesus loved the Bible.

Jesus was the most important baby to ever live. His life is an example to us of how God wants us to live and to love God and one another. He taught us how to pray the Lord's prayer, and about how God is everyone's Father. God is very happy when we talk to Him.

Jesus died when he was still a young man. Some people hated him and had him put to death. But that is not the end to Jesus' story, because he came back from the dead. On Easter Sunday morning, Jesus came out of his grave alive. It was a very exciting day.

He visited with his apostles and friends for over a month. Then he said good-bye and ascended into heaven. Jesus promised that one day all of us will live together with him and his Father forever.

PRAYER: Dear Jesus, please make your home in my heart and live there for ever and ever. Amen.

Supplies needed

saw

hot-glue gun

craft glue

silver, gold, or iridescent glitter

raffia

acrylic paint

2 pieces of fence post 2" in diameter (one piece 7½" long and one piece 6½" long)

1 piece of wooden dowel 1¼" in diameter and 4" long

1 short piece of wooden dowel, 1" in diameter

piece of firewood or tree limb that is approximately 2" in diameter

piece of firewood or tree limb that is approximately 3" in diameter

December 30 — Sunday within the Octave of Christmas
The Feast of the Holy Family

The Holy Family — Our Lord Jesus Christ, the Blessed Mother, and her chaste spouse St. Joseph — has always been regarded by the Church as the model for all Catholic families: the loving faith, obedience, and providence of the hard-working Joseph; the faith, love, obedience, and strength of the Blessed Mother; the perfection of the Son of God made Man, who submitted in obedience to a human mother and foster father. These perfect models lived a human life like ours, which makes it possible for us to seek to imitate their virtues. The feast of the Holy Family is celebrated on the Sunday that falls within the Octave of Christmas or, if no Sunday falls within the Octave, on December 30.

Rev. James Gaunt, C.S.B., crafted our wooden Holy Family from fence posts and broomstick scraps. It serves as a simple yet effective reminder of the solidarity of the Holy Family.

Wooden Holy Family
Directions

Cut fence post and wooden dowel to the lengths above to form the bodies of Joseph, Mary, and Jesus.

Slice two ½" thick slices from the 1¼" piece of dowel to make faces for Mary and Joseph, which leaves the baby's body 3½" long. Slice a ½"slice from the 1" diameter dowel for the baby's face. Haloes are 1" thick slices from a piece of firewood or tree limb; Joseph's halo is approximately 3" in diameter; Mary and Jesus have 2" diameter haloes.

Paint haloes yellow ochre. Paint a brown rim around the edge of the small circles that will be the faces; paint the faces flesh color. Paint Joseph's body brown; paint Mary's body blue-green; paint the baby's body white.

When paint is thoroughly dry, use a hot-glue gun to glue the pieces together as shown in the picture. First, glue the bodies of Mary and Joseph together at the sides. Then add their haloes and faces. Glue the baby's halo and face to his body; then glue his body onto the holy couple. Using white craft-glue and glitter, make a few lines on the haloes. Finish your project by tying the trio together with a raffia bow.

Wooden Holy Family

Special Occasions

Baptism

In the sacrament of baptism, the priest pours water on a person (or immerses him) and pronounces the words "I baptize you in the name of the Father, and of the Son, and of the Holy Spirit." The one baptized is cleansed of original sin and is incorporated into Christ and made a member of His body, the Church. He is infused with sanctifying grace and receives the theological virtues of faith, hope, and charity, and the gifts of the Holy Spirit, which enable him to receive the other sacraments effectively. A shell-shaped container, connoting Christian pilgrimage, is sometimes used to dip the water out of a larger container, then pour it on the baby's head.

You can make a beautiful yet simple shell that can be used during the ceremony and kept as a remembrance of that important day.

Supplies needed

a seashell, such as a large cockle or oyster shell, which could easily scoop up and hold a tablespoon of water

fine-line permanent marker

bottle of pearlized fabric paint

clear acrylic spray

Baptism Shell

Directions

Using the fine-tipped marker, carefully write or print the child's full baptismal name inside the shell. Write the date and the words "Holy Baptism."

Using the pearlized fabric paint, carefully pipe a line of paint all around the outside of the shell. Let paint dry overnight.

Finish by spraying several thin coats of clear, acrylic spray. This will make the natural colors of the shell look bright and wet. Be careful! If your first coat of spray is too heavy, the words will run. It is better to spray the paint in very, very light coats, allowing each to dry before adding the next.

Hint: If you don't live near the beach, ask a seafood restaurant to give you an oyster shell, look for one in a craft shop, or ask around among your friends who have been to the shore for vacation.

First Holy Communion

Traditions involved with the first reception of the holy Eucharist abound in all Catholic cultures. These have often changed or modified due to the fashion of each particular country and the different ages at which children generally receive the sacrament.

In the United States in the 1950s and '60s, First Communion classes received the sacrament in elaborate ceremonies with the children

Baptism shell

dressed all in white. The little girls wore frilly dresses and beautiful veils, making them seem as if they were miniature brides. Today, in most parishes the girls simply dress in their "Sunday best," and veils may be optional.

The exact origin of the wearing of veils for First Communion is shrouded in history. Among the Romans and early Christians, women always covered their head. Among Western Christians, the wearing of the bridal veil is all that is left of the distinctive veil of the married woman, common to many parts of the world and known long before Christianity. Head veils are still customary in many countries, especially where the Muslim religion predominates.

The Christian significance of the veil was its symbolism of marital fidelity. Its association with virginity was a later idea. Before the liturgical changes of the 1960s, all Catholic women covered their heads with some sort of head covering each time they entered the sanctuary. The Fourth Lateran Council in its consideration of Communion by children said only that children must be suitably dressed for the occasion. The tradition of Communion veils probably stems from each of these earlier customs.

If your parish still keeps the tradition of wearing veils at First Holy Communion, there is no need to purchase an expensive one from the store.

You can make an inexpensive and very attractive one easily. The same technique can also be used for veils for *quinceañeras* (the celebration of a young women's 15th birthday) or weddings.

First Communion Veil

Supplies needed

wire — any type that is easily bendable, yet stiff enough to hold its shape

plastic bags from the grocery store or produce department — white or clear (cut off colored part)

2 yards of 7/16" wide (#9) white floral ribbon (acetate satin)

1 yard of 72" wide tulle

hot-glue gun

needle and thread

2 white silk flowers, 3" in diameter; 1 yard of small pearls; piece of thin white ribbon (optional)

Directions

Form a circle of wire approximately 5" to 5½" in diameter. Take a plastic bag and wrap it tightly around and around the wire ring until you have used the entire bag; add another bag and continue wrapping until the entire circle of wire is covered and is about ½" thick. Secure with a tiny dot of hot glue.

(Careful, don't burn your fingers! Use the eraser end of a pencil to press the plastic onto the glue.)

Hold one end of the ribbon tightly against your padded frame and wrap it through and around the frame; continue wrapping until the entire frame is covered. Wrap the ribbon as tightly as possible. When the entire circle is wrapped with the ribbon, secure the end with hot glue and cut off any excess. Reglue if necessary to make certain the end is stuck down well.

Fold the tulle in half, width-wise, six times. You should have a rectangle that is 1 yard long and 4½" across.

Fold in half lengthwise. Now your rectangle is 4½"x18".

Place a saucer near the cut end of the tulle and, holding it firmly against the fabric, use a pencil to lightly trace the curved edge to the folded sides of the tulle. With sharp scissors, carefully cut along your line; this will make the scallops at the bottom of your veil.

Unfold the tulle and refold it lengthwise so that the top scallops are about 1" above the bottom scallops. Using a needle with doubled thread, make a small stitch to catch the thread about 1" below the folded edge, then baste along the width of the veil, 1½" below the folded edge. You can line the bottom scallops up with the edge of your counter or table to help you keep your basting line straight.

Gather tulle along the thread until a line measured from side to side along your stitching is 11". Place a couple of small stitches at the edge to secure. Even out the gathers and pin veil to circle with straight pins, leaving the prettiest, most even part of the circlet in front. The shorter line of scallops should be on top. With a needle and doubled thread, whip the veil into place on the circlet. Remove pins.

First Communion veil

Now that you have completed the basic veil, you have many options for the final touches: you can add ribbons, pearls, silk flowers, jewels, etc. In some parishes, all-white veils are mandatory; in others, a touch of color may be added. Whatever you choose to finish your veil, it should be in keeping with the communicant's dress.

We finished our veil by hot-gluing a yard of tiny pearls around the crown and adding two white silk flowers on one side.

The Quinceañera

The *Quinceañera*, or celebration of a girl's *quince años* — 15th birthday — is a Catholic celebration popular in Mexico and in those places in the United States where those of Mexican descent reside. Based on indigenous Mexican Indian rites of puberty, today's *Quinceañera* celebration marks a girl's passage to womanhood.

A special Mass and service provides an opportunity for the birthday girl to renew the promises made for her at baptism, to pray that God's graces will not be wasted in her, and she takes Our Lady as her model, her strength, and her guide. The priest reminds her that she is now the age at which Our Lady experienced the Annunciation, and that she, too, is now becoming a woman.

At the beginning of the Mass, the girl enters dressed in a long dress almost as elaborate as a wedding dress, but in her chosen color. She wears a long lace *mantilla* or other veil. Halfway through the ceremony, the veil is removed and the girl is crowned with a jeweled tiara.

Traditional gifts such as a Bible, prayer book, or a rosary are presented by her *Padrinos y Madrinas*, adult sponsors who help to arrange and pay for the ceremony. The girl is attended by a *Chambelán de Honor* — Court of Honor. In the United States, there are often 14 pairs of attendants, as well as the girl's escort; each pair marks one of her 15 years. Sometimes the attendants range in age from about five years old to the teenage years.

After the Mass comes a grand *fiesta*, or party, with food, champagne, presents, music, and dancing. *Mariachis*, musicians with guitars and trumpets, may serenade the girl, and she usually begins the dancing by taking the first turn with her father or uncle. A special cake is usually topped with a doll dressed in a replica of the girl's *Quinceañera* dress.

Today, Church professionals are paying more attention to the tradition of the *Quinceañera*. Some dioceses have issued guidelines on its preparation and celebration. Although some have suggested that the celebration has become too extravagant, others say that when families request a *Quinceañera* Mass, it is a teachable moment, a time for education in the faith. In its guidelines, one diocese recommends five preparatory sessions covering faith, baptism, and the meaning of the ceremony, and encourages total family involvement and participation.

Champagne Bottle Planter

The next time you attend a *Quinceañera* or wedding, ask for one of the empty champagne bottles. Take it home and craft a personalized planter that can be presented as a special gift to the birthday girl or newly-married couple.

Supplies needed:

champagne bottle, rinsed and dry

electric engraving pencil

cuttings of pothos ivy or heart-shaped philodendron

Directions

Using the same technique of glass engraving that you used to make the Holy-Water Bottle on page 59 of this book, carefully write the name of the girl or the couple in a pretty script in the center of the widest part of the bottle. Underneath the name, in slightly smaller letters, write the words "*Quince Años*" or "Our Wedding Day" (depending on whom it's for). Beneath that, engrave the date.

Fill the bottle with water. For optimum growth, add one or two drops of liquid fertilizer. Break off several long stems of a pothos ivy (or heart-shaped philodendron). Get the longest stems you can. Both these plants grow well hydroponically (water only). They thrive on a sunny window sill, but can be grown under artificial lights. Carefully pull the leaves off the bottom of the stem until you have a sprig with bare stem at least 6" long; the longer the better. You want the stem to reach down into the bottle where the bottle begins to widen; stems too short will result in your having to check the water level in the bottle too often.

Champagne bottle planter

Make certain each stem has at least two or three leaves left at the top. Three stems per bottle is sufficient. These ivies grow rapidly, so if you haven't got cuttings that are long enough, begin their growth in a wide-mouth glass and when your cuttings have grown to a sufficient length, pull off the excess leaves at the bottom and carefully push the stems and roots into your bottle.

Presenting this souvenir to the birthday girl a month or so after her *Quinceañera*, or to a newly-married couple a month or so after the wedding, makes a wonderful surprise and can bring back happy memories.

Weddings

A wealth of customs surrounds the wedding ceremony in every culture. Each ethnic group, each geographical region, has developed customs and styles peculiar to itself.

In Sweden, one of the items made for cooking that was also traditional for weddings was the cake or cookie stamp. Each family had a set of beautifully carved stamps to use for special holiday celebrations, weddings, and funerals. Guests at these functions were given small cakes stamped with their host's designs to take home. At Christmas, piles of little stamped cakes or cookies were made for all the members of the family. The stamps were round, square, or diamond-shaped, and cut into them were geometric patterns or figures of animals, birds, flowers, or hearts.

A girl's fiance would carve a stamp and give it to her as a token of his love. She would make him some cookies decorated with the stamp, called fiancé buns.

The custom of making cookie stamps is believed to have begun sometime in the early 16th century, and it reached its height during the 18th and 19th centuries. Some rural families have handed down stamps for generations that are still being used today.

Cookie stamps are also popular in Germany and Scotland, as well as a number of other regions in Europe. The stamps are generally carved from wood or clay. You can make a simple set of stamps for cookies or candy from self-hardening clay. Use them to make plates of cookies or candies for the next family wedding or other celebration.

Swedish Cookie Stamp

Directions

Supplies needed
Sculpey III clay
oven
waxed paper
cookie sheet
empty soda or other bottles
various kitchen implements

For each stamp, form a ball of clay about the size of a walnut. Place it on a waxed paper-covered table or counter and flatten it until you have a disc about ½" thick.

For a square stamp, use your thumb and forefingers to square off your disc. Roll out a ½" "snake" between your palms, and cut a segment about ¾" long.

Place the handle in the center of a disc and join together by sliding your finger down the side of the handle, bringing a little clay with it, to fill the crack at the base. Smooth around the join until it is complete.

Put your stamp, handle side down, on the top of a soda bottle and allow it to dry for several hours, until the clay has a leathery texture.

Cut a design into the bottom of your stamp using kitchen implements. Experiment to find which works best. A bottle opener, a grapefruit sectioner, or the eraser-end of a pencil all can be used to form designs. Linoleum-cutting tools are perfect, if you happen to have some; otherwise, check all the kitchen drawers for potential cutting tools.

Thin lines will not show when stamped on cookies; the best designs are simple, cut in deep, wide lines. Geometric patterns, flowers, holiday patterns, all can be used effectively.

Remember that initials must be cut in "mirror image" — reversed in both order and direction. A single initial usually makes a prettier stamp than attempting an entire word.

As you cut, remove any excess clay, and use your finger to smooth rough edges. Sharp edges are preferred, but sometimes the clay will "wrinkle" and need a bit of smoothing.

When you have several stamps completed, bake them on a foil-lined cookie sheet at 300° for 30 to 40 minutes. Allow them to cool thoroughly before use.

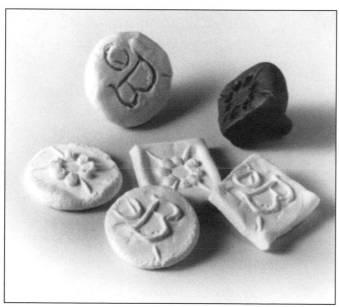

Swedish cookie stamps

Dessert Mints

You can use your stamps to decorate attractive candy mints using the recipe for Christian Symbols Candy found on page 135 of this book.

Supplies needed

waxed paper

candy dough

saucer

granulated sugar

cookie stamp

Directions

Break off small pieces of the candy dough and roll into a ball. Press the top of each ball gently onto a saucer covered with granulated sugar.

Place on waxed paper with the sugared side up. Stamp with your cookie stamp to form design. Allow to dry until hardened.

Aberdeen Scottish Shortbread

Real Scottish shortbread is another prime recipe for use with your cookie stamps.

Supplies needed

2 cups flour

2 sticks butter (½ pound)

½ cup granulated sugar

8"x8" cake pan

sharp knife

oven

Directions

Allow the butter to sit until it is room temperature. Mix in the sugar thoroughly. Add flour and mix thoroughly.

With your hands, pat evenly into the 8"x8" pan. Your shortbread should be nearly an inch thick.

Put pan in refrigerator to let dough stiffen a bit; at room temperature it may be too sticky to cut. When dough is stiff enough, cut into 16 pieces with a sharp knife.

Use your cookie stamps to stamp the center of each piece. Set oven to 300°. Bake shortbread about 50 minutes, or until it just begins to turn a golden color and you can smell an explosion of the delicious smell. When cool, recut along your lines and remove from pan. Serve with hot tea or coffee.

Ordination

The ordination of a priest is one of the most beautiful and moving ceremonies of the Catholic Church. Just as with any other major religious celebration, the commitment to the priesthood is one of joy for the candidate and his family. It often is celebrated with a meal or reception and the presentation of gifts.

You can make a small souvenir from his ordination for a favorite priest. Or remember an anniversary or jubilee in the same way. At many ordinations and jubilees, it is still customary to pass out a small prayer card with the date and occasion printed on the back. Take an extra card or, if none is available, purchase a small "holy card" from the religious goods store. Combine it with the old German custom of decorating religious pictures with pressed flowers to make a bookmark for your favorite priest's prayer book or Bible.

Pressed-flower Bible marker

Germany has a long history of flower-related arts. Pressed flower collections and flower drawings, paintings, and prints have been made for centuries.

Many flowers in Germany have symbolic meanings. Folk stories explain the origins of others. For example, the *edelweiss*, a particularly treasured flower that grows in the Alps, is associated with immortality, purity, and courage. An old folk tale relates that an angel wanted to visit the earth again and was allowed to take her human form and descend to the Alps. When a mountain climber discovered her and fell in love with her beauty, God transformed her into the *edelweiss*.

No one knows when flowers were first pressed in Germany as a way of preserving them. For many years it has been the custom to press flowers under heavy books and then to put them under the glass around the border of religious pictures.

Pressed-Flower Bible Marker

Supplies needed

ordination souvenir card(s) or holy card

small flowers and leaves

heavy book

brown paper bags

craft glue

stick

hot-glue gun

tweezers

scissors

heavy colored paper (not construction paper)

1 sheet laminating paper or clear Contac paper

3 colors of ¼" satin or grosgrain ribbon, 12" each

hole punch

Directions

Go on a flower hunt in your yard or a nearby field to locate tiny flowers and leaves suitable for pressing. Remember that a weed is only a flower whose virtues have not yet been discovered, so look to the lowly weeds for some lovely contributions to your pressed-flower collection. In the process of pressing, you will probably ruin some of the flowers and others will not hold their color well, so gather more than you think you need.

Cut pieces of paper from a brown grocery bag that will fit inside the pages of a heavy book. This is to keep from staining the pages of your book; some flowers bleed when dried.

Carefully lay your flowers between these pages and stack more books on top. You will need to let even the tiniest flowers dry at least a week. When flowers are thoroughly dry, you are ready to proceed.

Cut a 4"x6" rectangle from heavy, colored paper. Do not use construction paper, as this type of paper fades rapidly. Center the ordination or "holy" card on one side, with the picture showing, and attach it with a glue stick.

On the back, center and paste another ordination or holy card so that the text shows. If you do not have a card for the back, you can write a personal message by hand, or type or print it neatly on another color of paper and paste that on the back.

A pair of tweezers will help you lay your pressed flowers in a decorative manner around the picture on your card. When you are satisfied with your design, glue the flowers in place with the tiniest dabs of white glue. Allow to dry.

Laminate your card front and back with the laminating paper. This is tricky, so read the instructions that come with the laminating paper carefully. You may even want to practice on some other type of card first; it would be a shame to let this part spoil your entire project.

Cut your laminating paper larger than the card. Fold down the backing a bit and stick the laminating paper to a counter. Then carefully smooth the paper down and across the face of your card. Turn the card over and repeat the process.

Using the handles of your scissors, press down tightly all around the edge of the card to make certain the two pieces of laminating paper are tightly stuck to each other. Trim off the excess about 1/16" inch from the edge of your card; if you cut too close, the paper may peel away.

Carefully punch three holes across the top of your card. The top of each hole should be no closer than ¼" to the edge of the card. Space them evenly across the card; one in the center and one each equidistant from the center hole and the edge of the card.

Thread the end of one ribbon through a hole from the front and fold it up about ½" on the back. Attach with a spot of hot glue, using the eraser end of a pencil to press the ribbon together tightly until the glue sets. You may use craft glue for this, but the hot glue makes a better, more flexible bond and will stand up to use better.

Repeat to attach the other two ribbons. Carefully draw a thin line of craft glue or fabric paint across the end of each ribbon to keep the ribbon from fraying. Your finished bookmark can mark three separate places in the recipient's Bible or prayer book.

If you particularly enjoyed this craft, you may want to try a larger project. Using the same technique, you can press and glue flowers on a larger religious print.

Frame your work in a picture frame under glass as the Germans did.

Funerals

Through recorded history and in almost every culture, some sort of public ceremony has been held to commemorate the time of burial. From earliest times, flowers were used at burials. The ancient Greeks were buried in white robes and wreaths of flowers were presented by friends and relatives. Flowers were strewn about the funeral couches of the early Romans.

During the early Christian burial rites and commemorative Requiem Masses, flowers were occasionally strewn on the grave. Through the years, floral tributes of various kinds were popular in many places. In 19th-century America, evergreens were used to cover the exposed dirt at the cemetery before the mourners arrived; fresh flowers were used for a child's burial.

In El Salvador, the people *Enflorar a los Niños* — literally, flower the children — by covering the graves of children with flowers on November 1.

In many cultures, paper flowers are sometimes used to substitute for real ones. In some parts of Mexico, the making of paper flower *coronas* (crowns or wreaths) and *crucitas* (crosses) as decorations for the cemetery is considered an art. Placed on a grave, the paper flowers are more brilliant and just as fragile as their natural counterparts; the first rainfall destroys their beauty.

Florists sell the popular replicas of these traditional decorations from small shops lining the cemetery walls. Today's florists slap together *crucitas* and *coronas* using a hot-glue gun, silk flowers, and ribbon; the exquisite, handcrafted paper ones are difficult to find, as only a few craftsmen have learned the original art.

Our *corona* and *crucita* are made from brightly-colored tissue flowers formed in a manner simple enough for even small hands to make. They can be tributes for the cemetery, or can brighten up a spot on your wall at home. The flowers can be used for many decorative purposes.

Cut-Paper Corona *and* Crucita

Supplies needed

brightly-colored tissue

scissors

white glue

cardboard

plastic bags from the grocery
  or discount store

Directions

Remember that colored tissue is not a standard size. Start with a large *square* of tissue. Fold your square in half from top to bottom, then fold in half again from side to side. Continue folding until your paper is in a square with sides about 2½".

With the folded corner as shown in the diagram, cut according to either of the patterns shown for petals. Unfold. Don't be worried if your unfolded pieces aren't exactly round or perfect; when you are finished, you won't be able to tell.

From scraps, make centers by making thin slices across a rectangle, cutting almost to the edge. Cut leaf pairs from folded green tissue as in diagram. Fold your tissue several times to cut multiple leaves at a time.

Work at a counter that is easily cleaned or work over waxed paper. Wet tissue bleeds and the dye from the paper may stain furniture or clothes; it will wash off your hands.

Unfold and separate a number of your petal pieces. Place a tiny drop of white glue in the center of five or seven of your petal pieces. Place one of your flower centers on the drop of glue on a petal piece. Layer your petal pieces, turning each so that the petals are slightly turned and not exactly on top of one another. Using your thumb and first two fingers, pinch the center back of your flower together tightly.

Turn the flower a bit and pinch again until you have formed a point at the back of your flower. This will cause your petals to bunch out and resemble a flower. While the glue is still damp, you can use your fingers to fluff the petals to an attractive shape.

Add a pair of leaves with a tiny drop of glue at the back center of your flower. Set aside while you form more flowers.

Try mixing colors for a different type of flower; you can experiment with making larger or smaller flowers, but even the smallest needs at least five petal pieces to bunch together to form a pretty flower.

Top: cutting lines for flowers; Bottom left: centers; bottom right, petals

We used a dozen 5" flowers to form our 9" diameter *corona*; use 15 to 18 to form our *crucita*. Cut a base from corrugated cardboard.

Our *corona* is made on a circle of cardboard that is 9" in diameter; the base is 1½" wide. The bars of our cross are 1¾" wide; the cross is 15" tall with an 11" crossbar.

Cut green tissue in 3" widths from the end of the folded pack to form wrapping strips. Attach the end of a strip to the back of the *corona* (or *crucita*) with a small dot of white glue.

Crumple the plastic bags.

Cut-paper *crucita*

You can use newspaper if you don't have a surplus of plastic bags. Lay the crumpled filler on the front side of the *corona* and wind your wrapping strips over and around until you have completely covered the base. This will make the base a little puffy on the front.

Glue your flowers on the base with drops of white glue. You can begin at any point on the *corona*. For the *crucita*, it is best to glue a flower at the four points of the cross first. Then, using flowers of equivalent size, add to each arm in turn until you reach the center.

Cut-paper *corona*

Ancient Traditions

An Appeal to the Olfactory

An appeal to the olfactory nerve can stimulate memory and alter behavior. Modern science tells us that for people smells and memory seem to go hand-in-hand. Memories tied to scent are usually more vivid and immediate than those associated with the other senses.

The study of aromacology — a body of research on the behavioral effects of fragrance — suggests that fragrances can do a number of things, such as relieve stress, elevate mood, increase alertness, stimulate and suppress the appetite, and increase performance. More and more people are practicing aromatherapy; the adherents consider this an ancient art. Testing has begun on a large scale in Japan to measure the effects of subliminally-sensed aromas in controlled environments.

From antiquity, people believed that whatever delighted the human senses must also be pleasing to the gods. They also felt that through burning and the ascension of smoke, sacrificial offerings were transported into the realm of divinity. In another use, because modern sanitation was unknown and bathing was a luxury, incense, perfumes, and other appeals to the olfactory were popular as cover scents.

The earliest-known records of incense use are found in Egyptian hieroglyphics from the middle of the third millennium B.C. About 1500 B.C., Queen Hatshepsut sent a fleet to what is now part of northern Somalia to acquire frankincense and myrrh tree seedlings.

The royal hopes for immortality among the ancient Egyptians caused a great consumption of these two "perfumes of the gods," and one inscription reports that nearly two million pieces of frankincense were burned during the 31-year reign of Rameses III. When the tomb of Tutankhamen, who lived about 1340 B.C., was opened in the first quarter of our own century, the air inside still smelled of myrrh.

In Exodus, we read that in addition to the ten commandments, Moses brought down from Sinai specifications for the Ark and the Temple, directions for religious ceremonies, and recipes for sacred incense made with frankincense and sacred anointing oils based on myrrh.

The Magi brought costly gifts of gold, frankincense, and myrrh to the long-awaited Messiah. All were rare and costly commodities of the ancient world. Both frankincense and myrrh are aromatic gum resins — dried tree sap. The trees from which they come are found naturally only near the southern tip of the Arabian peninsula and the northeast corner of Somalia. For centuries they resisted all attempts at transplantation. The harvesting of the resins is a laborious process, even today, so they were scarce and thus valuable in the ancient world.

The harvesting and sale of these resins was strictly controlled by the rulers of the areas where the trees were grown, driving the price even higher. At the high point of the frankincense trade about A.D. 100, a pound of frankincense cost more than the equivalent of $500 in today's currency; a pound of the choicest myrrh was as much as eight to ten times that amount. An estimated three-thousand tons of these commodities was shipped annually to Greece and Rome alone.

Incense was apparently not a part of the earliest Christian worship. Some scholars believe the early Christians rejected its use because of its pagan connotations. During the Roman persecutions, Christians were ordered to offer incense before an image of the emperor or other pagan deity; those who capitulated were called *thurificati*, after the *thurible* or *censer,* in which incense was burned for this test of fealty.

Other scholars hold a simpler explanation of the lack of burning incense in early-Christian rites. Early Christian worship was secret. The strong odor of incense might have meant discovery and persecution. Thus, the Christian use of incense probably did not emerge until the reign of Constantine in the fourth century when the Church was free to practice its worship openly.

Incense, as it is still used in the Church today, is rich in symbolism. The rising smoke continues to suggest the ascent of the prayers of the faithful. The ritual censing of ecclesiastical objects symbolizes sanctification, and the censing of the worshipers not only implies sanctification but also celebrates their participation in the liturgical ceremony.

The way incense is actually experienced is another dimension of worship. Modern science has discovered that smell is the only sense wired directly to the limbic system, sometimes called the "old mammalian brain," which regulates vital autonomic functions, biological rhythms, and basic instincts. In short, our sense of smell affects the source of our most powerful emotions.

Potpourri, bath salts, atomizers, incense, and sachets can all be made for a delightful appeal to the senses.

Making Potpourri

Imagine a time when people bathed infrequently, didn't use deodorant, and wore the same clothes day after day. Homes had no running water and heating and cooking were done over open fires. Lights were tapers; lamps were made from animal fat. Sanitation was practically nonexistent; the family dog was most often found taking a nap under the table.

If you can imagine life as described above, you will readily understand why potpourri and other pleasant-smelling items were so valued in the Middle Ages. Many families

Potpourri

had their own "perfumery" where potpourri and other items were made and stored. Pleasant-smelling herbs were often strewn on the floors of homes and churches so that when trod upon a sweet odor was emitted that counteracted the myriad of olfactory offenders that stemmed from the everyday life-style.

The word potpourri comes from words literally meaning "rotting pot," which is an apt description of the original concoctions of the Middle Ages, where flower petals were mixed with spices and oils and kept in pots. These pots were opened when people entered the room in an attempt to freshen the air.

Today, you can purchase a number of inexpensive blends of potpourri to display in a pretty pot or bowl or to use in your craft projects. The most expensive potpourris rely extensively on flower petals; the least expensive contain extenders such as wood shavings that have been colored for looks. It's fun to make your own.

All potpourris contain three things: 1) flowers, leaves, and/or natural materials such as wood shavings, seed pods, etc. 2) Something to make the odor last, such as citrus peel or orris root. 3) Essential oils. A fourth item in many potpourris is spice — cloves, cinnamon sticks, etc.

For years I have kept a cardboard box on top of my refrigerator (remember, heat rises) where I put orange and lemon peels and flowers to dry. I hang herbs grown in my garden in bunches, leafy part down, from the ceiling above my kitchen counter. Last Christmas, my sister gave me a wooden rack for this purpose. Citrus slices dry well when suspended from this rack. You can make a good drying area in a corner of your garage or storage room. An old window-screen placed on tin cans to raise it from the ground or counter makes a good place to dry flowers and leaves; citrus slices or bunches of herbs or other natural materials can hang from a rafter in the garage; pick plants in the early morning and tie bunches with string around the stem end and hang upside down.

Floral Potpourri

3 cups dried flower petals and heads

¼ cup dried lemon peel

1 tablespoon lavender flowers

1 tablespoon ground orris root

15 drops lemon oil

5 drops rose fragrance oil

You can look for natural components for your own potpourri in a variety of places: your garden, nearby field or wooded area, grocery store, your house (old dried flowers from bouquets or arrangements), the workshop floor for wood shavings. We have made "sentimental" potpourri by drying the flowers in bouquets received on special occasions, such as the birth of a new baby. Oils and other special items, such as orris roots, may be available at a herbalist shop, a health food store, or in the potpourri section of the grocery store. If all else fails, a mail-order source is given in the list at the back of this book.

Today, many blends of potpourri oil are readily available, pre-mixed. If you have perfume oil, you can use this; using cologne or perfume rarely works. If you have a batch of old potpourri that has lost its smell and you don't know what the original oils were, you can place it in a zipper bag and shake with a teaspoon of Everclear or brandy. Allow to sit in a closed bag for a few days before use.

Save the peels from any citrus fruit eaten or used. Remove the white pulp and tear the peel into small pieces. Dry on your screen until hard.

Prepare citrus slices by cutting a lemon or orange into thin, ¼" slices. Using a regular sewing needle and thread, carefully sew a loop through the rind of each slice, so you can hang the slice where it will be exposed to air on all sides. Let the slices dry, preferably in a cool, dark area until they are hard and completely dry.

Once your peel has dried, if you want more color, you can put several drops of food coloring with a little water in a small jar. Drop in some of your peel, close the lid, and shake the jar vigorously a few times. Take the colored peel out and drain it on paper towel; allow it to re-dry thoroughly.

A simple, basic way to make to make potpourri is to place your dried mixture in a large bowl and add spices and extenders such as citrus peel and/or orris root. Mix thoroughly with your hands. Pour the mix into a large plastic zipper bag. Add a few drops of essential oil; seal bag and shake thoroughly. Allow your mix to "set" in the bag for a few days, preferably in a cool, dry, dark area such as a closet.

After a few days, open the bag and give it a "nose" test. If the odor pleases you, your mix is ready, although it can be stored in the closed bag until time for use. If you don't care for the smell, add a few more drops of one of the oils you used, re-shake, and test again in a few days.

You can try the recipes on the two pages that follow, or experiment with your own blends.

Spicy Potpourri

1 cup dried carnation petals and flowers

1 cup dried orange peel

½ cup dried red chili peppers (from produce section of grocery store)

2 tablespoons star anise-pods

1 tablespoon senna pods

1 tablespoon whole cloves

1 tablespoon ground orris root

5 sticks cinnamon bark, approximately 2" each, broken in pieces

20 drops sweet orange oil

10 drops sandalwood oil

Homemade Air Freshener

You can make an air freshener that is cheaper, more environmentally friendly, and which works as well as, if not better than, the commercially packaged sprays.

Supplies needed

small spray bottle with capability for fine mist

essential oils

water

Directions

Get a spray bottle from the cosmetic department of your local grocery or pharmacy. You want one that will spray a fine mist. Fill your bottle with water. Add a few drops of your favorite essential oil or oil mixture. To use, shake bottle and mist inside a room whenever you want a nice smell. Make certain you mist only over things that aren't hurt by water.

Try one or all of the following oil combinations:

10 drops lemon and 5 drops rose fragrance.

10 drops lemon and 2 drops lavender.

8 drops sweet orange and 6 drops sandalwood.

8 to 10 drops patchouli (this fragrance is strong; don't mix with anything else)

Relaxing Bath Salts

Aromatherapy is in! The water-softening effect of the salt plus the delicious aroma and cool color of the water makes for a luxuriously relaxing bath.

Supplies needed

large coffee can or jar with lid

ice cream salt

blue or green food coloring

perfume oil, potpourri oil, or essential oil

clear plastic-wrap

ribbon

small bowl or basket

card for directions for use

Directions

Put ice cream salt in a large coffee can or jar, leaving several inches of space at the top. Add a few drops of green or blue food-coloring, cover container with lid, and immediately shake vigorously to distribute the color throughout the salt. The longer and harder you shake, the more the color spreads.

Next add several drops of your favorite oil; repeat the shaking. If the odor isn't strong enough, add a few more drops and shake again.

If you like, make a batch of blue and a batch of green, then mix the two. In only a few minutes you have made a batch of bath salts as good as any you can pay a fortune for at the store!

For a gift, fill a small basket or bowl with your bath salts. Wrap in clear plastic wrap and tie with a ribbon for the finishing touch. Attach a small card with directions to pour a tablespoonful under running water for a luxuriant bath.

Hint: Plain table salt will work as a base, too. Just remember to let it dry on a cookie sheet before packaging. Pack this in a pretty bottle instead of a basket or bowl.

Cologne will not work to fragrance potpourri. Look for essential oils where potpourri is sold or at an herbalist's shop; at the grocery, some oils are available in the cake and candy section. Lemon and lavender oils make for a refreshing bath; rose oil is relaxing; peppermint stimulates.

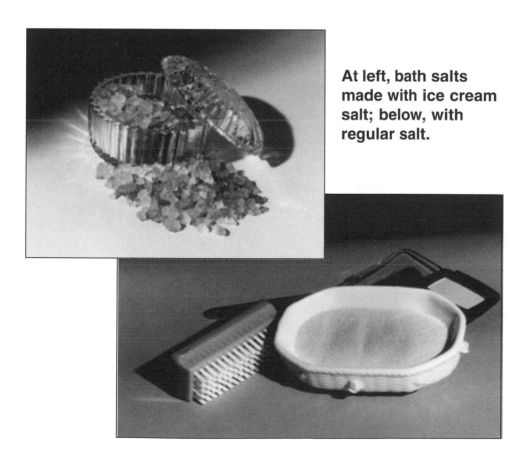

At left, bath salts made with ice cream salt; below, with regular salt.

Symbolism and Secrecy

Until the reforms of Constantine, Christianity was largely a religion practiced in secret. Persecuted by the pagan Romans, the Church literally went underground; for the first two centuries the Christians held their religious rites in underground cemeteries called the "catacombs."

In the Roman catacombs, the walls near places where martyrs' bodies rest are usually covered with inscriptions called "graffiti." These writings belonged to the faithful, who wanted to leave a memorial of themselves close to the martyrs' remains or, more often, those of their deceased friends and relatives. Usually the graffiti consists of the names of persons, accompanied by a wish for salvation in the next world.

The graffiti soon took on the form of cryptographic writing, whereby the Christians could secretly express their feelings and the highest ideas of the Faith in a brief and effective form during times of persecution. Many of the Christian symbols we are so familiar with today had special meaning for those early, persecuted members of the Church.

Throughout the centuries, Christian artists have made use of the rich tradition of symbols to embellish ecclesiastical art. Many monograms and letters have symbolic meanings, as do pictures. The early Christians often used the fish sign to indicate the direction to a meeting or to identify each other. A number of Greek and Roman letters are made into monograms for Christ or abbreviations for religious concepts. To early Christians, a bird was a symbol for the human soul; pomegranates symbolized the Resurrection, as did pelicans. A rose is symbolic of Our Lady.

There are numerous forms of the cross, each with its meaning. In addition to the symbols given in the Appendix, there are a wealth of others which can enhance your projects. Your city or church library is a good place to research this subject to find symbols that especially seem to fit your own designs.

Christian Symbols — Art to Eat

An excellent class project for Catholic schools or religious education classes that are studying Christian symbols is to make the symbols out of candy clay. When dry, the candies can be taken home, discussed with the family, and eaten!

Directions

In a large bowl, mix the powdered sugar and cream cheese (soften to room temperature first). Mix with hands until a stiff clay is formed. Add flavoring oil (*not* extract) a drop or two at a time, kneading into the clay until the dough is flavored to taste.

Separate the clay into as many sections as you want for different colors. Color by adding cake coloring one drop at a time and working through the clay.

Supplies needed
1 box powdered sugar
1 small package Philadelphia cream cheese
flavoring oil
food coloring

For the lesson, discuss how Christian symbols can remind us of important ideas about our Faith. Discuss the Early Christians' use of secret symbols. A heart reminds us of love. The early Christians used a fish to identify each other. A star announced the birth of Jesus. Display several simple patterns of symbols. Refer to the patterns on pages 157-59.

Give each of the children a piece of the candy clay and a piece of waxed paper to work on. Have them form their favorite symbols with the clay. Let them harden on the waxed paper. Then eat your art! Or take it home to share the lesson and the goodies.

Hint: Peppermint, spearmint, cinnamon, and orange oils are usually readily available in the candy-making section of a department store or in the grocery or drug store. Some oils are stronger than others; be careful with peppermint and cinnamon.

Icthus Napkins

The fish is one of the oldest and most widely-known symbols of Christianity. The Greek letters that mean Jesus Christ, God's Son, are usually found imprinted on this symbol. They are written as: "ΙΧΘΥΣ" or "ΙΧΘΥC" and pronounced "*I*ota *Ch*i *Th*eta *U*psilon *S*igma." The "C" is the older form; "Σ" is more modern.

Supplies needed

light-colored cloth napkins (or use men's handkerchiefs)

fish-shaped sponge for printing

stiff brush

acrylic paints

bottle of iridescent fabric paint

bottle of blue-green glittery fabric paint

cardboard box

waxed paper

straight pins

Make our attractive *Icthus* napkins to decorate your dinner table and provide a symbolic reminder of your Christianity.

Directions

Secure your napkins to the cardboard box with straight pins, putting a layer of waxed paper between the box and the napkin. Thin a little light-blue paint with water.

With a stiff brush, paint a swathe to simulate water about 3" from one corner of the napkin.

Using yellow, yellow ochre, or pale-orange paint, cover the top of your sponge with a thick layer of paint. Carefully print the fish on the napkin, letting his lower fins slightly overlap the blue swathe. Push down the sponge carefully with your fingers to ensure a clear print. You can cover tiny flaws with your paintbrush.

When the paint is thoroughly dry, outline the fish with the iridescent fabric-paint and write the word "ΙΧΟΥΣ " across the body of the fish.

Make a few random squiggles of the paint on the water to simulate ripples or waves. Using the blue-green fabric-paint, put a dot to form the fish's eye.

Carefully personalize your napkin with the recipient's name. Allow the fabric-paint to dry overnight before disturbing; the longer it dries the better the paint will set.

Hint: Purchase a pre-cut fish-shaped sponge or make your own. To make, draw a fish-shape on a regular household sponge with pencil. Use scissors to cut your design. If you wish, use a hole punch to punch out a hole for the fish's eye.

Icthus napkins

Symbol Bead Jewelry

Beads are known in all cultures throughout history. Made with all types of material, beads have often found eccliastical uses. Special beads meant to be sewn on altar fabrics were made in Russia and decorated with religious motifs. Our symbolic bead jewelry combines the Russian decorative-motif with the look of Italian *majolica*, Venetian glass beads, and an African trade-bead design.

Directions

Working on waxed paper, form beads from modeling compound. To make beads with variegated colors, roll thin "snakes" of the clay and twist together; break off pieces and form into beads.

Our brown and white *majolica* round beads are about ½" in diameter and a little over ¼" thick. The varicolored Venetian beads are slightly smaller.

The oval *Chi Rho* bead is ¾" long and slightly over ¼" thick. It is hung with two flat beads ½" in diameter and ¼" thick. The *Chi Rho* pendant is a teardrop-shape that is 1½" long made from white clay with an edging and the *Chi Rho* made of brown clay pressed onto the white base.

The cross pendent is a rounded triangle 1½" tall and 1" wide at the base. The cross was made of yellow clay and pressed on the triangle.

Supplies needed
Sculpey III modeling compound — brown, white, pink or red, green, and yellow
toothpicks
waxed paper
cookie sheet and oven
clear acrylic-spray
silver paint pen
2 small, plastic-coated paper-clips
white nylon twine
green nylon twine

Make holes in the beads with a toothpick; insert pick through bead from one side and then the other to make holes more even. This type of clay does not shrink when baked. Bake according to directions, about 20-25 minutes in a 275° oven.

When beads have cooled, spray with a light coat of clear acrylic-spray. Take your time and turn the beads to coat each side. Use a silver or gold fine-point paint-pen to draw Christian symbols on the beads. When dry, finish according to directions and the illustrations on page 138.

Majolica earrings

Carefully bend the smaller, center part of white-coated paper-clips out and down. Straighten out this part and slip on a bead. Bend the wire back toward the hook and wrap once around the base of the hook. Fold any excess downward against the back of the bead. If there is too much wire left, cut it off with a small pair of wire cutters.

Tear-Shaped Necklace

String the tear shape on white nylon cord, and slide to the middle of the cord. Tie a knot close to each side of the tear shape. Tie a knot ½" from the first knot on each side. Slip a bead onto each side and make a knot close to the outside edge of each bead. Continue in this manner until you have three beads on each side. Try on the necklace, pulling it up and down until you find a length that suits you. Holding the cord tightly together in the back, make certain the necklace

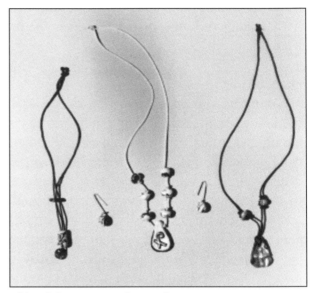

Necklaces and earrings

will slip over your head easily. Join the strings with a tight knot at the end. Using a cigarette lighter, slightly burn the end of the cords to make certain they will not unravel and cause the knot to untie.

Chi Rho Oval Bead Necklace

Thread a piece of green nylon cord through one of the flat, washer-type beads and center on the cord. Run both ends of the cord from the bottom to the top of the long, oval bead with the raised *Chi Rho* symbol, then through the second flat bead. Measure, tie, and burn the ends of the cord as above.

Cross Necklace

Make a loop in the center of a piece of green nylon cord. Push the loop from back to front through the hole at the top of the triangular cross pendant. Push both ends of the cord through the loop and pull tight against the pendant. Tie a knot in each cord about 1½" from the pendant. Slip a bead on each side and tie another knot close to the outside edge of each bead. Measure, tie, and burn the ends of the cord as above.

Old Testament —
Noah's Ark Wreath

Christians everywhere have celebrated the story of Noah and God's promise, symbolized by the rainbow in story, song, and handcrafts. Many of you may have a play-set of the ark and the animals, treasured from childhood. We crafted a door wreath to remind us of this happy Bible story.

Directions

Most craft stores carry preformed straw wreaths. You can make your own by cutting a large circle of cardboard and tying handfuls of straw to it with clear fishline. Cut a coat-hanger and secure carefully to the back of the wreath for a hanger.

Unfold 1 yard of blue paper twist and wrap tightly around a segment of the wreath at the bottom. Secure with glue and floral or hair pins. Attach the ark to the wreath on the blue segment with florist wire and pins with a little glue for stability.

Supplies needed

Noah's ark play set

large, straw wreath — purchased or made

blue paper-twist for bow

floral wire

hot-glue gun and glue

coat-hanger

rainbow suncatcher

acrylic paints

small wirecutter

floral pins or large hair pins

Noah's ark wreath

Unfold another yard of blue paper-twist and make 3 to 5 loops under the ark to simulate water, overlapping the loops slightly and securing with pins. Put several drops of hot glue on the bottom of the ark and push the "water" loops up to cover the bottom of the ark.

Unfold a third yard of paper-twist and tie a large bow, securing it under the "water" with glue and pins.

Glue Mr. and Mrs. Noah on the ark. Paint the rainbow suncatcher with opaque acrylic paints. If you can't find a rainbow-shaped suncatcher at your craft store, cut a rainbow shape from heavy cardboard or thin wood and paint with the acrylics. If you use cardboard, paint both sides to seal the rainbow and make it watertight (important if you plan to hang your wreath on an exterior door).

When dry, center the rainbow at the top of the wreath and hot-glue it in place. Hot-glue the animals around the wreath as if they were entering the ark.

Noah's Promise Tote and Tee

Supplies needed

plain, white tee-shirt

and/or

colored-fabric totebag

acrylic paint

stiff-bristled brushes

straight pins

cardboard

waxed paper

typing paper for pattern

scissors

pencil or chalk

1 package Crayola painting sponges — animals

fine-line, black, permanent marker (optional)

bottle of iridescent fabric-paint (optional)

patterns from the Appendix

Directions

Place a piece of cardboard inside your shirt or bag with a piece of waxed paper in between the fabric and the cardboard. Pin with straight pins to keep fabric from moving about while painting.

Cut a rainbow-shape from a piece of paper using the pattern provided in the Appendix, page 175; trace the shape on your totebag or tee-shirt in the top, left area. Use a pencil to trace the pattern onto white fabric; chalk or a dressmaker's marker works for colored fabric.

On colored fabric, first paint the entire rainbow area with white acrylic paint, straight from the tube or jar; don't thin the paint. With a stiff-bristled brush use short strokes to outline and fill in the outline. Allow to dry.

Paint the rainbow with acrylic colors straight from the tube; don't thin. Start with a red band for the top or outside band. Then, in order, paint bands of orange, yellow, green, blue, and purple. Each color should not vary in width, but the different colors do not have to be exactly the same width. For example, the yellow band may be a little wider than the others and the purple may be narrower, as mimics nature. Allow to dry.

Thin the acrylic paint with a small amount of

water and paint the top of an animal sponge, making a thick coat of paint. Print the animal on your project by setting the sponge, paint side down, carefully in position and pushing down with your fingers. If part of your design does not print, you can fill in the spot with your paintbrush. It's a good idea to practice your printing technique on a scrap of fabric or paper before actually printing on your project.

Add as many animal prints as you wish; choose your own colors. Use the shapes from the Appendix, page 174. If you like, when the paint is thoroughly dry, you can add details such as eyes, or outline your animal stamps with either black permanent-marker or iridescent fabric-paint.

Projects should dry several days before wear or use. Wash in cold water.

Hints: See the section called "Sources," page 181, for sources of Crayola sponges. You can make your own painting sponges by cutting animal shapes out of inexpensive sponges.

Inexpensive tote bags are sold in crafts stores and fabric stores. You can make your own from sturdy fabric such as denim, unbleached muslin, or sailcloth.

Noah's promise tote and tee

Fund-Raisers

Traditionally, Catholic churches and schools have relied on the added income from fund-raisers such as bazaars to bolster their annual budgets. A craft booth is generally a favorite at these events, and all manner of handmade items are offered for sale. A number of the crafts in this book serve as good items for crafts booths. This section contains several other items that can be made relatively inexpensively, but which are attractive or unique enough to make good sales items.

Clothespin Cheerleaders

Supplies needed

old-fashioned clothespins (not the kind with springs)

saw

sandpaper

acrylic paints

fine-line, black and red, permanent markers

pom-pom drapery edging in your school colors

scraps of felt in school colors

needle and thread

scraps of yarn for hair

scraps of thin, 1/8" plywood

hot-glue gun

These cheerful school-spirit dolls are popular at school bazaars or fund-raisers and make nice table decorations for school athletic functions. See the diagram on page 144 for help in putting the clothespins together.

Directions

Carefully cut off 1" from the double end of the clothespin. Sand rough edges.

Choose a small piece of thin plywood for a base. Sand rough edges.

Glue the cutoff pieces at shoulder height of the doll to form arms. To make it seem if doll has her hands outstretched to the side, attach the rounded end to the body. To have her hands go forward, attach the flat side to her body, with the end you cut off pointing towards the back.

With acrylic paint, paint the base a solid color and paint her shoes and socks according to the diagram. Paint 2 light-pink cheeks on her face. Make 2 white dots for eyes.

Paint a short-sleeve shirt on doll. You can paint on a bib and suspenders in the same color as the skirt, or cut them from felt and glue on doll. Allow paint to dry thoroughly.

When paint is dry, carefully finish the eyes with the black, thin-line marker. Draw a mouth with the red marker. Dolls are cutest if you do not attempt to make a nose.

Glue scraps of yarn on your doll's head for hair. Be as creative as you like; some can have curls, some can have braids.

Clothespin cheerleaders

Cut a rectangle of felt 1" wide by 5" long. With a needle and thread, baste along the top of fabric and pull thread to gather material. Begin in the center of the doll's back and glue the top of the skirt around the doll's waist. Lap fabric over slightly and cut off excess. Run a line of glue down the edge where the skirt laps over and glue the top piece to the bottom.

Glue doll's feet to base. Glue 2 pom-poms cut from drapery edging to form cheerleading pom-poms.

Clothespin Angels

Tiny Christmas tree ornaments or angel dolls can be made from clothespins as above.

Directions

Unravel white braid or use a bit of cotton to form white hair. Blouse and top of skirt is painted white; skirt is formed of white felt and lace scraps.

Cut wings from clear plastic and draw a line of silver or

Additional supplies needed

white braid

lace scraps

piece of stiff, clear, plastic cut from soda bottle or box top

silver and iridescent fabric-paint

base or loop of cord for hanging

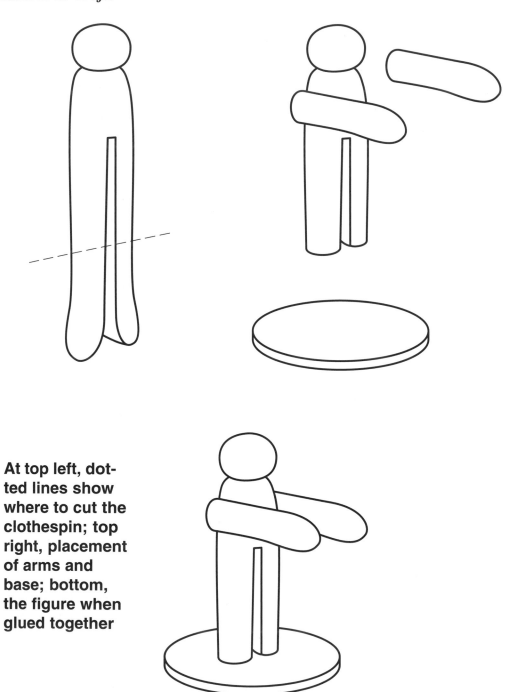

At top left, dotted lines show where to cut the clothespin; top right, placement of arms and base; bottom, the figure when glued together

iridescent fabric-paint around the edge. Make a few squiggles to indicate feathers. Allow paint to dry overnight before gluing on wings.

Cut a small rectangle from stiff, white, paper for a songbook. Edge with iridescent fabric paint. Allow paint to dry before attaching.

The halo is formed from a simple circle of metallic pipe cleaner. Glue on hanger or base.

Glass Paper Hair Ornaments

Attractive, yet simple to make and inexpensive.

Supplies needed
metal bases for barrettes
large, plastic chignon-pins
colored tissue paper
white glue
hot-glue gun
clear acrylic spray-paint
clear glitter (optional)

Directions

Form tiny flowers 1" in diameter from brightly-colored tissue-paper according to directions on page 124.

With hot-glue gun, attach flowers securely to barrette bases or to plastic chignon-pins.

Take your projects outside. Working over newspaper, spray the flowers on the barrettes and hairpins with an extremely light coat of clear acrylic. Allow to dry—paper dries rapidly. Continue spraying very light coats until the paper turns clear and looks like glass.

If you wish, you can sprinkle on a little clear glitter while the final coat of spray is still wet.

Angel in a Jar

Joanna found a fairy in a jar in a Florida flea market, but decided she'd rather keep an angel in a jar. On her last trip home, she showed me how to keep an angel in a jar on my own shelf.

Glass paper hair ornaments

Supplies needed

quart-size canning-jar (or other large, wide-mouthed jar)

flesh-colored Sculpey III or Fimo clay; mix colors for darker flesh tones

aluminum or easy-to-bend wire (not plastic-coated)

scraps of ribbon, lace, and net

12" piece of silver braid

bottle of glittery silver or iridescent fabric-paint

2" length of silver pipe-cleaner

stiff (yet flexible) clear plastic, such as that cut from a box lid

cotton balls

tiny beads for eyes

clear fishline

hammer and large nail

hot-glue gun

red, fine-line marker or drop of red paint

silver foil stars

Directions

Form an armature for your angel from wire similar to our diagram. It is about 3" tall.

Using Sculpey II or Fimo clay form a head and the hands and feet on the armature. Bake according to the directions for the clay.

When cool, glue on a dress of ribbon, net, or lace scraps. Place a tiny dot of red paint for mouth or use a red marker. Glue on cotton hair and a silver pipe-cleaner halo.

The angel holds a silver-foil star; silver-foil stars are also stuck to a piece of cotton "cloud" at bottom of jar.

Tie a piece of clear fishline around angel's body just under the arms, leaving one end about 5" long. Tie on a belt of silver cord.

Cut both wings as a single piece from clear plastic. Edge wings with glittery silver or iridescent fabric-paint. Allow to dry thoroughly before gluing them to back of angel with hot glue.

With your hammer and nail, make some holes in the jar-lid so your angel can breathe!

When your angel is complete, suspend it about halfway down in the jar. Fold the fishline over the lip of the jar and screw on the lid tightly. Your angel appears to be flying inside the jar.

Finish by tying a silver cord around top of jar.

Angel in a jar

Top left, wire armature for angel form. At top right, shapes for head and hands to be made from clay and placed on the wire. Below, pattern for wings; can be enlarged.

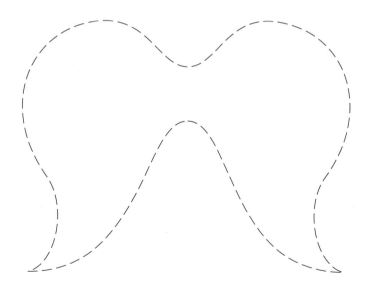

Patchwork Vase

Supplies needed

clear wallpaper-paste

magazines with shiny pages

waxed paper

scissors

bottles of metallic gold or silver fabric paint

empty vigil-candle glasses or attractively-shaped glass bottle

What Catholic church doesn't have leftover glasses from the large vigil-lights? We found a pretty and practical way to recycle them as patchwork vases.

Directions

First, clean and dry the vigil-candle glass or glass bottle.

Cut small triangles from magazine pages; triangle sizes may vary, but none should have sides longer than 2". Work on a counter that's easy to clean, or over waxed paper; this is a messy project!

Glue triangles to glass with the wallpaper paste. Begin at the top of glass, letting a small part of the triangle lap over into the inside to cover top rim. If you are using a bottle or jar with a screw-on lid, you may want to circle the top with a piece of folded paper to cover the ridges. Continue gluing on triangles until entire glass is covered. Let paper lap under base a little to make a finished edge for the bottom.

Allow vase to dry.

Using the fabric paint, go back and outline as many of the triangles as you can. When fabric paint has dried overnight, give your project a final coat of clear spray if you like.

Make an arrangement of silk, paper, or dried flowers to fill your vase as a gift for a girl friend or female relative. A small vase made in masculine colors makes an attractive pencil holder for a favorite boy or man.

Home Hospital Nuns

In pioneer days, intrepid women religious trekked through forests and

Patchwork vases

across deserts to found hospitals for the service of God's people in America. From the first days of our country until today, dedicated sisters in the medical field have brought healing, comfort, and solace to millions of Americans. We salute their ongoing efforts in Catholic hospitals across the United States.

Make this pair of sisters to remind you of their loving care, and to care for minor headaches and bumps at home.

Keep Sister Koolie on hand for those bumps and bruises that require the soothing coldness of ice. Fill her habit with ice and lay her on the "boo boo." Tears dry fast and swelling recedes under her cool care.

Have a headache? Stuffy head and sinus problems? Sister Soothie with her relaxing lemon/lavender scent comes out of her plastic bag to the rescue! Lie back for a few minutes, close your eyes, put your feet up, and rest Sister Soothie on your head. Soon you'll breathe easier and your headache will fade away. Or simply use her as a sachet, or, unscented, as a soft toy for a little one.

Directions

See the diagrams in the Appendix, pages 176-77, for help in putting the sisters together.

Cut tags off of washcloths.

Cut a small cardboard oval approximately 2" long and 1½" wide to form the back of the sister's head. Place the oval about 1½" from one corner of a rag and put a little stuffing between rag and cardboard to puff out face.

Gather fabric to the back and stitch down, making the center of the drawn-together fabric about ¼ of the way down from top of oval (see figure #2).

Along the side edges, make a tight fold approximately ½" wide. Fold over and over toward the front (approximately 5 folds) on each side to form arms.

Temporarily secure with straight pins. Bring arms to front as in figure #4. Sew across arms tightly, about 2" beneath the chin, sewing through the arms but not the back of the fabric.

Remove pins.

Supplies needed

4 thin blue washcloths

small piece of cardboard or stiff plastic cut from soda bottle

needle and thread

elastic thread

cotton or stuffing for heads

scissors

straight pins

lavender essential oil

lemon essential oil

zipper-lock plastic bag

small scraps of non-ravelling fabric (such as felt)

bottles of fabric paint

For Sister Coolie:

Working from the inside, carefully whip across the arms all the way from top to bottom. Fold triangular flap at bottom up to bottom of arms and sew securely to arms; do not sew through to back of doll. This will leave two oval openings at the base of doll.

Using a needle threaded with a double strand of elastic thread, sew around the openings just at hem of cloth, pulling fabric together slightly. Finished bottom will have two small openings that you can stretch open just enough to slip in an ice cube.

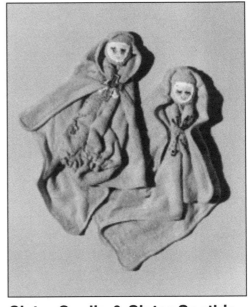

Fold a corner down 1½" and under and place on head for veil. Sew across top of veil to approximately ¼ of the way down on each side of head. Tack veil in at side of arms. Sew securely.

From the fabric scraps, cut a small cross about 1½" by 1" and an even smaller one about ¾"x½" for Sister Koolie to hold in her hands and to end her rosary. Tack in place.

Make face as shown in diagram

Sister Coolie & Sister Soothie

on page 177. Using light-pink fabric paint, draw a half circle and fill it in. Use yellow ochre for oriental sisters; light brown for African-American or Hispanic sisters. Add round cheeks and mouth in a darker pink.

Let paint set for a few minutes before rimming face with white. Allow doll to dry overnight before attempting to paint on eyes.

Sister Koolie's hands are teardrop shaped, painted with the same color as her face. Her crosses are outlined and the rosary is painted with dots of iridescent gold.

For Sister Soothie:

Make face and veil in same manner as Sister Koolie. Paint on rosary with iridescent gold. Using green paint, draw stems and leaves for her bouquet. Then add three large flowers and make dots of a contrasting color for the smaller flowers. Center large flowers with a dot of yellow or gold. Allow to dry overnight.

Place 8 to 10 drops of lemon essential oil near Sister Soothie's bouquet. Add 4 to 5 drops of lavender flower oil.

Seal Sister Soothie in a plastic zipper bag. She should be stored in the zipper bag until someone with a headache or stuffy nose calls. The drawer she is stored in will take up her soothing scent. Her odor will last for several "cures" if stored in a tightly sealed bag; refresh by adding more oil as needed. If she is made for a gift for a friend, mix a small amount of the oils and present a tiny bottle of the mix along with Sister Soothie.

Jesus Loves the Little Children

Jesus loves little children. He reminded his disciples that it would be better for someone to be cast into hell than to harm a child. He would not let his followers keep the children away from Him. He said, "Let the children come to me, and do not hinder them; for to such belongs the kingdom of heaven" (Matthew 19:14). He reminded us that we must become like innocent and trusting little children.

Having been raised a Protestant, my childhood memories of church revolve mainly around Sunday school. Classrooms held a myriad of toys and games to occupy us while the adults attended to the serious business of "attending church."

There was no Sunday school, of course, for Sunday evening services, so I sat in the pew beside my grandmother and never next to my brother. Our minister talked a long time, and I was an especially wiggly kid. To keep me quiet and in order to keep my hands busy, my grandmother would occasionally let me have a throat lozenge or antacid tablet from a tin in her purse. To this day, a taste of either of these brings back a flood of memories.

Toys in church were forbidden, but when the wiggles got too much, my devout grandmother would pull out her hanky and, at the same time she was paying careful attention to the minister, fold the hanky into baby Jesus in his swaddling clothes. Then she would unfold it and hand it to me. How I tried to copy her folds! What she did so simply was beyond my grasp for years. When I would finally give up, she would refold the hanky and I would spend the remaining few minutes of the sermon cuddling the simple hanky doll. By the time I learned how to fold the hanky myself, I was old enough to listen to the sermon! When I began working on this book, I remembered my "hanky"

Jesus, and that is how I worked out the pattern for the home hospital dolls in this book.

A good idea for mothers, grandmothers, or godmothers to make and present to a favorite small child is a Mass bag. This bag stays hidden all week in Mother's room and only comes out when the child attends Mass. The bag is filled with soft and silent toys that can occupy small minds and fingers so the adults can more fully participate in the Mass.

Decorate a small tote bag for this purpose, or use the Noah's Promise Tote from page 140. Add a favorite child's religious

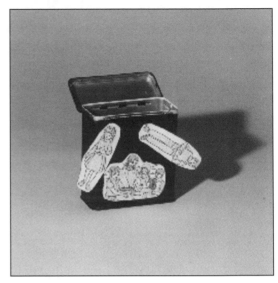

Jesus in a tin

book, Jesus in a tin, and the pillow baby Jesus doll from page 107 of this book. Other good choices would be a small plastic rosary or St. Thérèse's Good Deed Beads found on page 85.

A small child won't, of course, know the significance of the beads, but pulling them up and down the string can keep little fingers busy for quite a while. Making a child's visit to church a pleasant experience will help to ensure that the child grows to love it.

Supplies needed

empty Band Aid tin

spray enamel

MagicCard peel-and-stick business-card magnets

copy machine

small, sharp scissors

colored pencils

Jesus in a Tin

A good item for a small child's Mass bag is a tin with magnet cutouts of Jesus, the children, and the priest.

Directions

Save an empty Band Aid tin. Carefully spray-paint the tin a solid color. The best colors to cover the lettering printed on the tin are black, red, and dark blue.

MagicCard peel-and-stick business-card

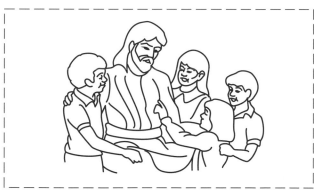

These pictures can be copied, cut out, colored, and affixed to the magnets. They can be enlarged or reduced on a copier to fit your need.

magnets are found in large office-supply stores and some crafts shops. If you have difficulty locating them, a number to call for the supplier closest to you is listed in the sources section on page 181.

 The cards are sold in small packages, so you can use the leftovers for other craft projects. Your local craft shop may also carry an equivalent type of magnet; if you use the thin tape strips you will need to glue your patterns to heavy paper.

Copy the patterns on page 153 onto a sheet of plain white paper (can be enlarged or reduced on a copier to fit your need).

Color the pictures with colored pencils.

Cut the patterns out on the rectangle and affix to the magnets as per the peel-and-stick directions on the magnet package. Then carefully cut out each piece on the inner lines. Pack pieces in the tin and slip tin into your child's Mass bag.

Supplies needed

plain white baby tee

bottle of fabric dye

salt

rubber bands

Tie-Dye Baby Tee

Babies can go "styling" as well as grown ups! Make this tie-dye tee for your favorite little one.

Directions

Wash or rinse tee to remove the sizing in the fabric. Work on a waterproof surface.

While tee is still damp, pinch up pieces of the fabric all over the shirt and twist a rubber band very tightly around the piece of fabric you have pulled up.

Continue until you have rubber-banded many parts of the shirt. You can make tight folds in the shirt and rubber band around them for a different effect.

Following directions given on the bottle, boil water in a sauce pan on the stove and prepare the dye. Remember to add salt as called for in the directions.

Dip the shirt in the dye and leave it the required amount of time, simmering and stirring.

Rinse the shirt first in warm water, then cool, keeping the rubber bands on the shirt. When the water runs clear, you have rinsed enough.

Hang your banded shirt to dry. Do not remove the rubber bands until the shirt is completely dry; this may take 24 hours. Do not dry in a dryer. When shirt is dry, carefully snip off the rubber bands and unfold shirt. Rinse in clear water and hang, unfolded, to dry again.

Tie-dye baby tee

Appendix

Christian Symbols to Use as Patterns

The symbols on the next three pages can be enlarged or reduced on a copier to fit your need.

1. *Chi Rho* (Constantine Cross) — The cross said to have appeared in a vision to the emperor Constantine before the victory of Milvian Bridge, A.D. 312. It is composed of the two initial Greek letters of the name of Christ, entwined as a monogram (Christogram).
2. (Not shown) Cross — Universal symbol of the Christian faith (use number 14, Celtic cross, without the circle behind it).
3. Crown — Symbolizes victory and sovereignty.
4. I.N.R.I. — The initials of the Latin version of the inscription written by Pilate and placed on the cross: Jesus of Nazareth, King of the Jews.
5. JHVH — Jehovah — the Christian form of the name given to the Hebrew name of deity, consisting of the four letters JHVH, never spoken by the Jews. Translated as "The Lord" in the King James version of the Bible.
6. Star of the Epiphany — Star which guided the Magi.
7. IHC or IHS — The first three letters (*iota, eta, sigma*) of the Greek spelling of Jesus. The first form is more ancient; the second is more common now.
8. ICTHUS — Sign of the fish; from the Greek letters IXOYC, meaning Jesus Christ, God's Son.
9. Trefoil — An ornamental design of three divisions or foils such as a clover leaf, used as a symbol of the trinity.
10. Dove — Symbol of the Holy Ghost.
11. Host — Symbol of the body of Christ as used in Communion.
12. *Alpha* and *Omega* — First and last letters of the Greek alphabet. Used together, they symbolize the everlasting nature of Christ's divinity.
13. Anchor — Symbol of Christian hope.
14. Celtic cross — Used in northern Europe as a symbol of Christ's passion; the circle behind the cross arms denotes the everlasting divinity of Our Lord.
15. Star of David — Six-pointed star, symbol of God the Father; Jesus was born of the house of David.
16. Triuna — Symbol of the Trinity.
17. Ship — Symbol of our heavenward voyage.
18. Egg — Symbol of the Resurrection because it contains new life.
19. Dove with olive branch — Symbol of peace.

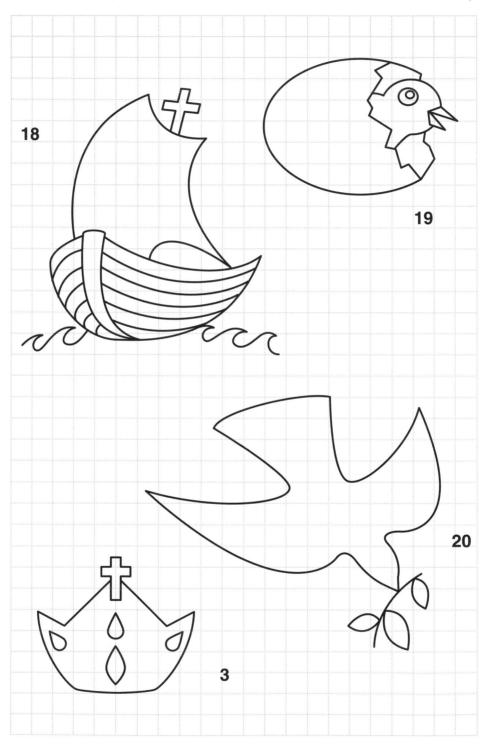

10

11

12

13

16

15

17

1.
Jesus is condemned to death.

2.
Jesus accepts His cross.

3.
Jesus falls the
first time.

4.
Jesus meets His mother.

5.
Simon of Cyrene helps Jesus
carry His cross.

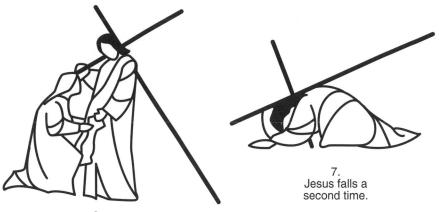

6.
Veronica wipes the face of Jesus.

7.
Jesus falls a
second time.

8.
Jesus meets
some women
from Jerusalem.

9.
Jesus falls a
third time.

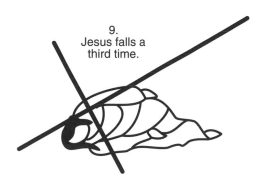

10.
Jesus is stripped of His garments.

11.
Jesus is nailed to
the cross.

12.
Jesus dies
on the
cross.

13.
Jesus is taken down
from the cross.

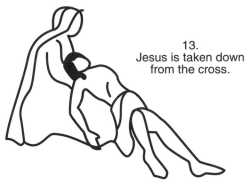

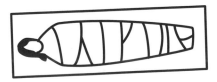

14.
Jesus is laid in the tomb.

15.
Jesus is raised to new life.

St. Ignatius

N. Sra. de la Manga

Mary (as Our Lady of the Sleeves [Sorrows])

Mary

St. Patrick

San MARTIN

St. Martin

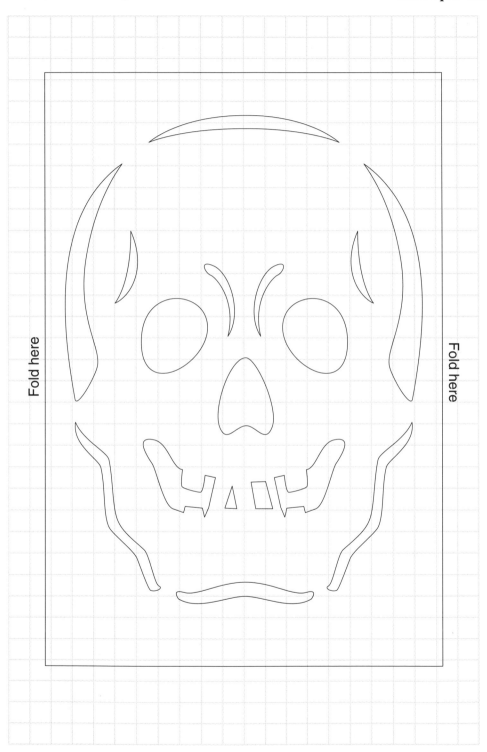

Fold here

Fold here

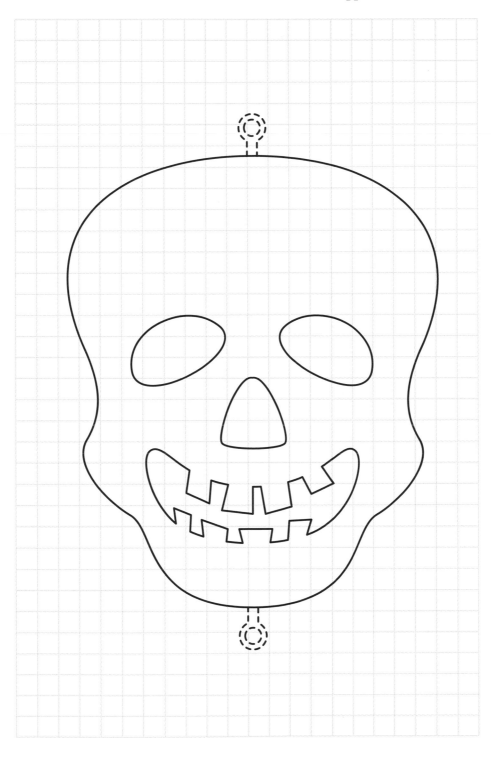

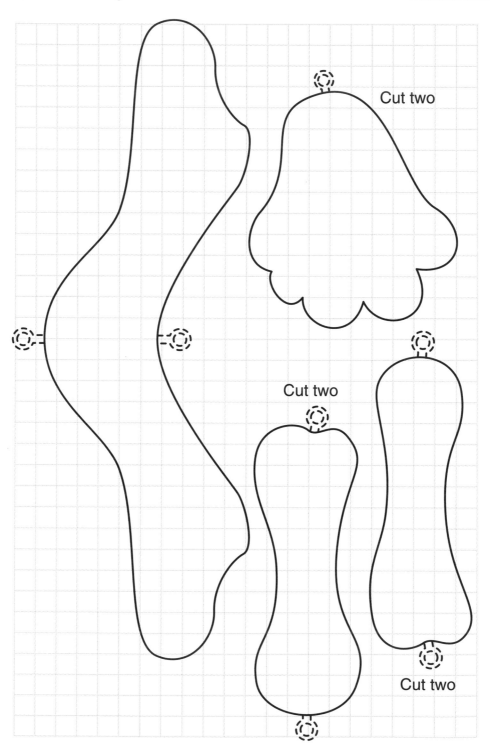

Cut two

Cut two

Cut two

Cut two

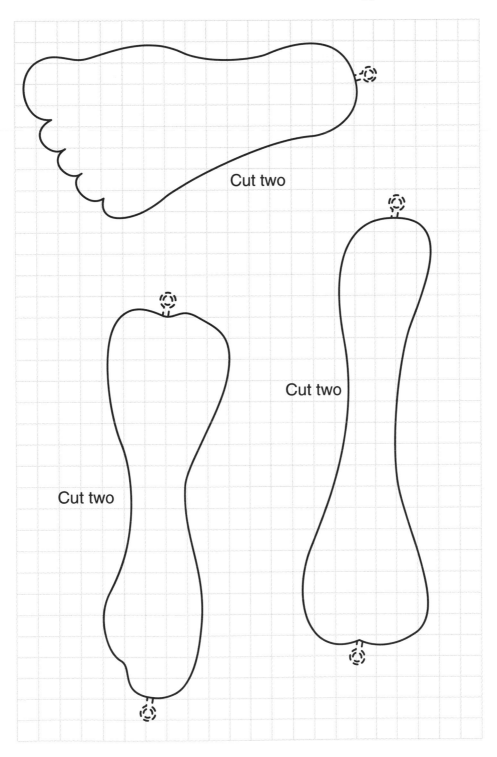

Cut two

Cut two

Cut two

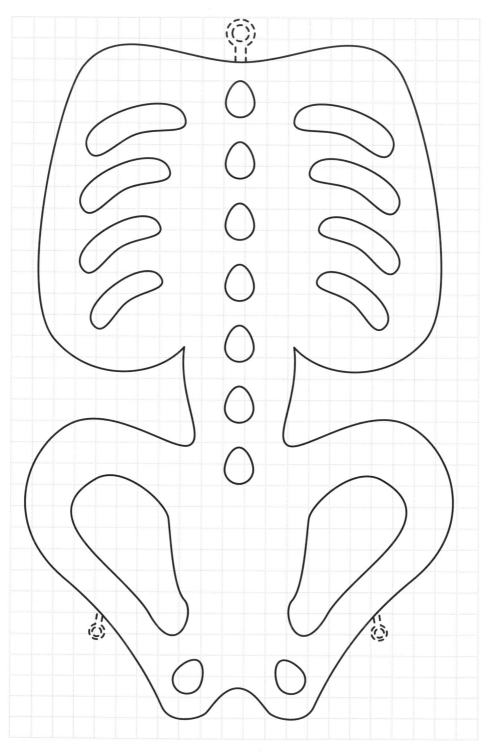

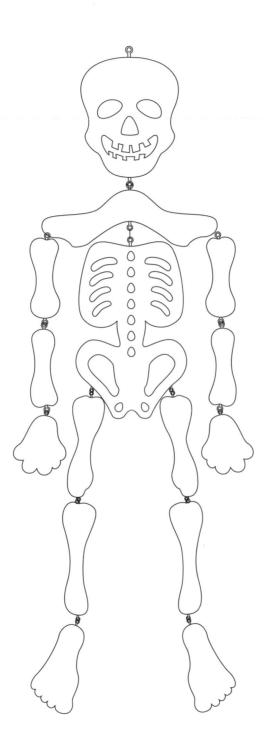

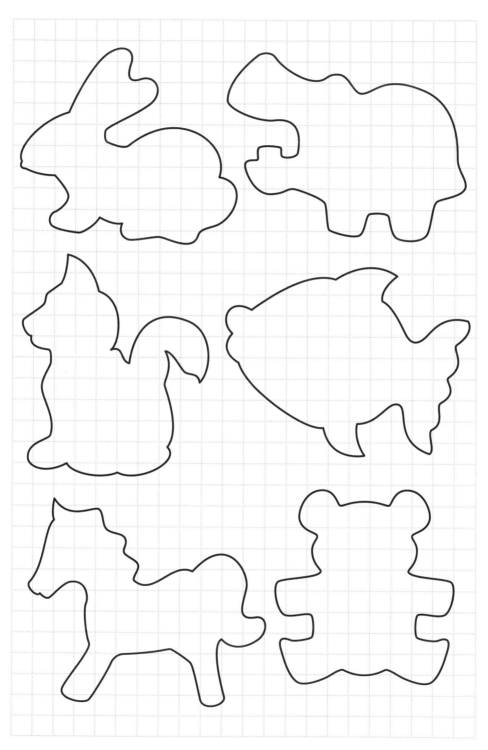

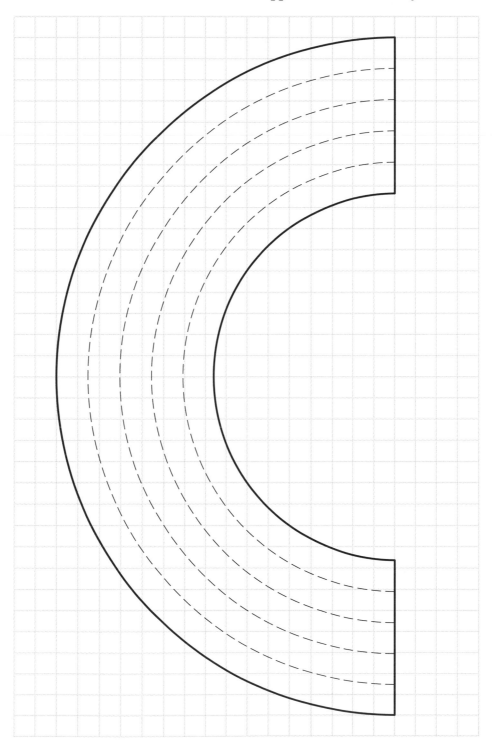

1

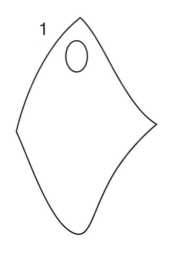

2

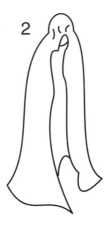

3

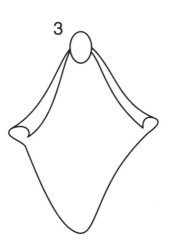

4

5

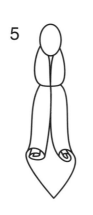

6

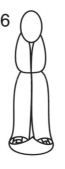

7

8

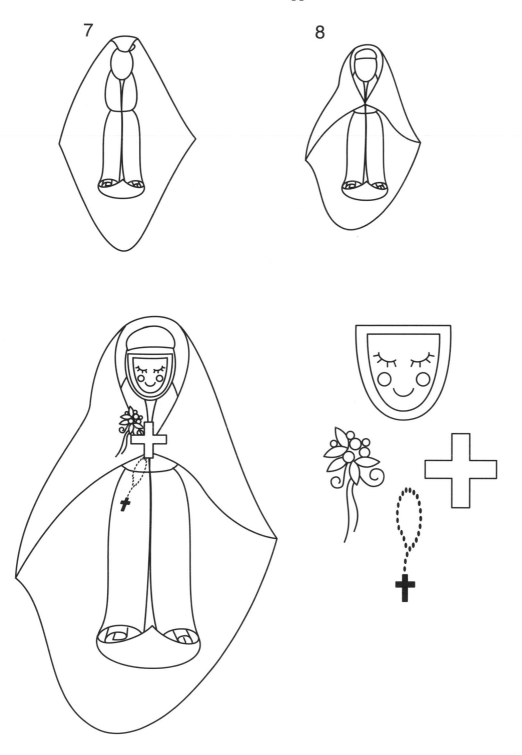

How to Enlarge or Reduce a Pattern

The simplest method for enlarging a pattern is to use a copy machine with enlarging capability. Just key in the percentage you want to enlarge it, and press copy! Presto! Same for reducing.

Many of our patterns can be used actual size or increased to 110%. If you can't get to a copier, use as is; the difference is minimal. Measure the items you're working with; measure the pattern; and size accordingly. If you need to increase a pattern to twice as large or more, and can't get to a copier, old-fashioned graph paper can do the trick. Here's how:

The original pattern is drawn on a grid with small squares (check out any pattern in the Appendix). Then a grid with larger squares is used to enlarge the original pattern. The size of the enlarged version depends on the relative sizes of squares on the two grids. Example: if you want your design to be twice as large as the original, your large squares must be two times the size of the original square. The size of the grids in this book is one-quarter inch; to make twice as large, your larger squares should be one-half inch.

Starting at one corner of the original pattern, the small squares should be numbered consecutively. First in a horizontal direction across the top and then in a vertical direction across one side of the design. These numbered squares will be used for transferring the design to a the large grid.

To draw a corresponding large rid of squares, you will need a large sheet of tracing or craft paper. Draw a horizontal and a vertical line intersecting at the top left-hand corner to form a right angle. Begin marking off large squares from left to right. Mark off as many squares as are on the small grid of the provided pattern. Repeat down one side. Draw lines horizontally and vertically to complete the new, large grid. Number squares to correspond to small squares.

To transfer the enlarged design, carefully copy the outline from the original grid, square by square. Use the numbered squares as a guide in transferring pattern. Be sure the proportion in each square remains the same on the enlarged version.

To reduce a pattern, simply reverse the procedure for enlarging the pattern. Instead of making squares larger, draw smaller squares on the corresponding grid, then copy from the original grid, square by square.

How to Transfer a Pattern

Keep the article as flat as possible when transferring a design. Always position the design in the best place, then secure the pattern with tape, pins, thumbtacks, or other suitable ways.

Carbon paper can be used to transfer patterns to paper, cloth, wood, and other surfaces. Dressmaker's carbon is better than office carbon paper, because it doesn't smear. Choose a contrasting color of carbon paper, so you can see it. Insert the carbon paper between the design and material, face down. Trace around the design with your pencil or pen, transferring the pattern as you work.

Templates: These are used when a series of shapes are going together to make one design or when a repeat pattern is needed. Templates can be made of plastic, wood, cardboard, or heavy paper. Transfer the design to the cardboard (or whichever material you choose). Cut out. Position on the area of the material you're working with, then trace with pencil, pen, or chalk.

Basting: This method is good for transferring designs on cloth to be embroidered or used with some kind of stitchery. Transfer the design to tracing or tissue paper. Pin in position on fabric. Stitch along the outline, taking small running or basting stitches. Carefully tear away paper, leaving stitches in place. Remove stitches as you work.

Tracing: If the fabric or paper is transparent, simply lay fabric over the design, secure, then trace, using pencil, pen, or chalk.

Sources

We hope you will be able to easily find sources close to you for all materials and supplies called for to create the crafts in this book. The following sources have indicated a willingness to help you in locating supplies, or to provide them by mail.

A Moveable Feast has a large selection of materials for potpourri and essential oils. Write or call them at (713) 528-3585 to inquire about products and prices. Address: 2202 West Alabama, Houston, TX, 77098.

Binney & Smith's consumer communications department can provide where-to-buy information and answer any questions about their products. Telephone 1-800-CRAYOLA.

MagicCard Peel 'n' Stick Magnets — Call 1-800-634-5523 to locate a source of the magnets in your area.

Pearl Art Discount Center — 1-800-221-6845. Located in eight states, call for mail order pricing on art supplies.

The Fitzgibbon Company is a Catholic religious goods and gift store. Write or call them at 1-800-352-0033 to inquire about prices for small medals, crucifixes, religious prints, etc. Address: 609 Fifth Street, Sioux City, Iowa 51101.

Thanks

My thanks to the following people, who have helped in so many ways in preparation for this book, by giving me ideas, suggestions, trying the projects, and most of all by their prayers and best wishes for its success.

Danielle Ball, Friendswood, Texas
Joanna Ball, Eglin AFB, Florida
Mary Bednars, Buffalo, New York
Davie Burleigh, Houston, Texas
Birdie Burleson, Huntsville, Texas
Heather and Glynn Burleson, Houston, Texas
Charlie Carrillo, Albuquerque, New Mexico
Father William F. Clark, O.M.I., Director, Missionary Association, National Shrine of Our Lady of the Snows, Belleville, Illinois
Norma Contreras, Houston, Texas
Rosemary Cushing, Omaha Urban Council of Catholic Women, Omaha, Nebraska
Judy Divon, Manvel, Texas
Julie Douglas, Jacksonville, Texas
Army Emmott, Houston, Texas
Lorraine Grandinetti Featherston, Tomball, Texas
Reverend James Gaunt, C.S.B., Manvel, Texas
Brother Paul Halaburt, New Melleray Abbey; Peosta, Iowa
Mary Ellen Hall, Houston, Texas
Sister Julia Hurley, Albany, New York
Sister Mary Agnes Karasig, Summit, New Jersey
Sister Eileen Ann Kelley, SP, archivist, Sisters of Providence, St.-Mary-of-the-Woods, Indiana
Leo Knowles, Manchester, England
John Laughlin, Huntington, Indiana

Jackie Lindsey, Huntington, Indiana

Karin Murthough, Houston, Texas

Reverend Z. Pazheparampil, S.J., Christ the King Major Seminary, Nyeri, Kenya

Pat Rensing, Los Angeles, California

Elsie Sanford, Jacksonville, Texas

Julianne Sanford, Jacksonville, Texas

Gjon Sinishta, R.I.P., Albanian Catholic Institute, San Francisco, California

Josyp Terelya, Toronto, Canada

Bebe Velez, Houston, Texas

William Velez, Houston, Texas

Billie Walter, Jacremba, California

Joannes Zheng, Beijing, P.R., China

Selected Bibliography

There is a wealth of "how-to" crafts books and myriad beautiful art-books that discuss the various traditions in crafts. For the serious crafter who is interested in learning new techniques and making new projects, books in this bibliography that contain instructions are marked with an asterisk (*). Other books listed served primarily as resources for the text.

*Andrew, H.E. Laye. *The Arco Encyclopaedia of Crafts*. New York: Arco Publishing Company, 1978.

Appleton, LeRoy H. *American Indian Design and Decoration*. New York: Dover Press, 1971.

Ball, Ann. *A Litany of Saints*. Huntington, Indians: Our Sunday Visitor Press, 1993.

Ball, Ann. *Catholic Traditions in Cooking*. Huntington, Indiana: Our Sunday Visitor Press, 1993.

Ball, Ann. *Handbook of Catholic Sacramentals*. Huntington, Indiana: Our Sunday Visitor Press, 1991.

Baker, Joan Stanley. *Japanese Art*. London: Thames and Hudson, 1990.

Bieler, Ludwig. *Ireland, Harbinger of the Middle Ages*. London: Oxford University Press, 1963.

*Coles, Janet and Budwig, Robert. *The Book of Beads*. New York: Simon and Schuster, 1991.

Daniels, David. "The History of Holy Smoke." *Catholic Digest*. St. Paul, Minnesota: University of St. Thomas, April 1995.

Dyan, Ruth. *Crafts of Israel*. New York: Macmillan, 1974.

Ekiguchi, Kunio, and McCreery, Ruth. *A Japanese Touch for the Seasons*. New York: Harper and Row, 1987.

_____ *Faberge 1846-1920*. London: Debrett's Peerage Ltd., 1977.

Guarducci, Margherita. *The Tomb of St. Peter*. New York: Hawthorne Books, 1960.

Gudio, José. *The Arts of Spain*. New York: Doubleday and Co., 1964.

*Harvey, Marian. *Crafts of Mexico*. New York: Macmillan Publishing Co., 1973.

Hottes, Alfred Carl. *1001 Christmas Facts and Fancies*. New York: A.T. DeLa Mare Company, 1946.

*Logan, Elizabeth D. *Shell Crafts*. New York: Charles Scribner's Sons, 1974.

McLanathan, Richard. *The Pageant of Medieval Art and Life*. Philadelphia: The Westminister Press, 1966.

NCCB. *The Book of Blessings*. New York: Catholic Book Publishing Company, 1989.

Osborne, Harold. *The Oxford Companion to the Decorative Arts*. Oxford: Clarendon Press, 1975.

Russel, Francis, and the editors of Time-Life Books. *The World of Durer*. New York: Time Inc., 1967.

Sayer, Chloë. *Arts and Crafts of Mexico*. San Francisco: Chronicle Books, 1990.

*Sayer, Chloë. *Crafts of Mexico*. Garden City, New York: Doubleday and Company, 1977.

Schuman, Jo Miles. *Art From Many Hands*. Englewood Cliffs, New Jersey: Prentice-Hall, 1981.

Sietsema, Robert. *European Designs*. New York: Hart Publishing Co., 1978.

*Singer, Margo and Spyrou, Mary. *Textile Arts, Multicultural Traditions*. Radnor, Pennsylvania: Chilton Books, 1989.

*Stribling, Mary Lou. *Crafts from North American Indian Arts*. New York: Crown Publishers, 1975.

Weiser, Francis X. *Handbook of Christian Feasts and Customs*. New York: Harcourt Brace and World, 1958.

*Wing, Frances S. *The Complete Book of Decoupage*. New York: Coward-McCann, Inc., 1970.

Index of Crafts

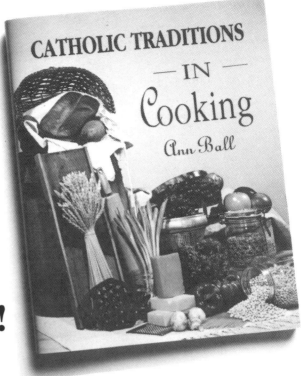